ASCENSION
CODES

ASCENSION CODES

The Little Book of Light Codes
VOLUME 2

*Activation Symbols, Messages,
and Guidance for Awakening*

LAARA

Publisher: Peacock Wisdom Publishing
ISBN (Paperback): 9781777351533
ISBN (Hardcover): 9781777351557
ISBN (eBook): 9781777351540

*This book is dedicated to
every being in search of truth
and the Love That You Are.*

Table of Contents

Acknowledgments

I am grateful to have the loving support of family, friends, and readers. A special thank you to my parents, Chuck and Alison Herod, my partner, Dr. Stewart Blaikie, my amazing editor, Michael K. Ireland, and my assistant, Janet Beardshaw. Thanks to my friend Ben Lott for his invaluable guidance and support. Thanks to all of my clients and students who encourage me to reach for new levels on my journey.

To my amazing teachers, Rosalyn L. Bruyere and Ken Weintrub, I appreciate deeply all that you have and continue to share with me.

To my Spirit Team, Master Ling, K, Lady Isis, and Jeshua, and all the Light Beings who support the healing and advancement on Gaia, my heartfelt Love and gratitude.

To the amazing team at Grammar Factory, and Geoff Affleck, thank you for your talents and support.

To my dear readers . . . thank you for your bravery and openness, and your ambition to heal and to raise your vibration and the planet's. I am honored to share these sacred messages with you.

LAARA

Foreword

As a lifelong advocate of the human experience, particularly when it comes to exploring the profound non-physical aspects, such as light, I was exhilarated by the profound journey I embarked upon in *The Little Book of Light Codes Volume 2*.

Having spent many years lecturing about the elements of nature, with a special focus on the transformative power of light, I eagerly embraced this book, seeking to expand my understanding of Light Codes and delve deeper into my personal gnosis. I have always held Laara in high regard and eagerly anticipated the opportunity to learn from her.

This remarkable book serves as more than mere reading material; it is a spiritual development course that will profoundly impact all who venture into its pages. It beckons us to "do the work," guiding us through the intricate pathways of Light Codes with the grace and clarity of Laara's words. She has masterfully presented these complex concepts in an easily digestible manner, despite the inherent unfathomable nature of Light Codes.

Within the ceremonial framework of the book, you will encounter Light Codes that offer a transformative experience, allowing you to delve into the hidden crevices of your being that often remain unexplored or undiscovered.

For me, this journey felt like venturing into uncharted territory. As I immersed myself in the Codes, what initially appeared as small discoveries soon revealed themselves to be expansive realms beyond my initial perception. It became evident that these experiences transcended the boundaries of imagination, inviting me to touch, listen, see, feel, and interact with an entire world unto itself. At times, this exploration dissolves into a wordless state of being, transcending the constraints of earthly realms and ushering you into an experience beyond the limitations of time and space.

Laara guides you precisely through this extraordinary journey, starting from the depths of your own being, as I described earlier. But the journey does not end there. With enhanced self-awareness comes an expanded awareness of the interconnected field to which you belong. Laara adeptly connects you to your guides, the planet, the universe, and ultimately, the Divine. This awareness of connectedness, both within oneself and with the entirety of existence, forms the foundation for a healthy life and a thriving society. I firmly believe that this book contributes to our collective evolution.

Each Light Code holds its own unique experience. As you read Laara's words, she skillfully guides you through their meaning and significance. And in the next moment, you may find yourself ascending into a wordless encounter, directly experiencing the essence of the Light Code.

I extend my heartfelt invitation to you to fully embrace the energy of these Codes and allow them to imprint upon you their essence. Open yourself to the transformative power they hold, and may you become one with the light that permeates all.

With boundless anticipation,
RA OF EARTH

Preface

Welcome to the next installment of the powerful book of channeled messages and symbols, *The Little Book of Light Codes*. As I brought *The Little Book of Light Codes* together in 2019, I knew it was a powerhouse of energy, but I didn't know how many lives it was going to change for the better. The book has been an incredible presence in my life, one I didn't understand until recently. It has shaped and directed my life's purpose in ways I could never have imagined. I have been inspired to travel the world to share Light Codes with amazing people through speaking engagements, spiritual events, and interviews. I've shared the wonders of Light Codes through social media, online events, and podcasts. In my self-development and practice, the Light Codes provide me with profound support. Even if this book is sitting on a shelf collecting dust, undeniably, it holds sacred energy.

The stories and messages I receive from readers touch and amaze me... from shifting and releasing old energy... to new sensations... to increased perception... to the way their animals respond to their owners reading *The Little Book of Light Codes* and *Light Codes for the Soul* to them! I never tire of hearing these sweet, special, and often profound accounts.

These are just some reasons I am so delighted to bring you this new compilation of sacred symbols and messages.

The Little Book of Light Codes Volume 2: Ascension Codes takes us on yet another journey, focusing on a deeper expansion of our consciousness.

When we can stretch our minds, connect with our hearts, and feel into the multidimensional nature of all things, we become happier and less concerned with the day-to-day nuances of life (which can be tiresome and limiting sometimes). Each symbol provides insight and guidance and nudges you closer to the Godhead.

Channeling this collection of symbols and messages has been both powerful and touching. I hope you will experience the same power and sentiment when you work with them. This book is imbued with an abundance of Light so each of us can remember, reclaim, and stand firm and confident in our true purpose.

Thank you, dear reader, for joining me on this ascension journey. I am humbled to share with you these energies, wisdoms, and healings for the upliftment of humanity and the discovery of self. It is a privilege to connect with Jeshua, Lady Isis, Master Ling, K, and the expanded team of Light Beings who assist me, Gaia, and the collective consciousness. I hope you revisit these Light Codes and messages often as intuition guides you. May you discover new ways to work with the Codes and experience new connections and energies. May your Love grow stronger within your being every day, and may Divine Light bless each day.

I wish you an enjoyable journey through this book—may you rediscover on the most profound levels the truth of who you are.

LAARA
The Tigress of the Light

Glossary of Terms

Adamantine particle: the smallest particle in existence, which is made of and responds to Love. For more information, please refer to *Love Without End* by Glenda Green.

Ancestral healing: the energetic healing of our family lineage, which can include multiple past, present, and future generations.

Aura: the electromagnetic field (biofield) produced by a living thing that surrounds the body.

Authentic self: the aspect of one's consciousness aligned to Universal Truth.

Centaurian: the energies and consciousness emitted from the star system pertaining to Alpha Centauri

Coherent energy: energy within and around our being that is smooth, integrated, and neutral.

Divine, the: another term for God/Source/Universe.

divine: pure, Loving energies of a sacred nature.

Ego: an important and helpful human aspect for keeping us safe, and in our soul's quest to learn about itself. However, it is common for most human beings to allow the ego to have power over our incarnated experience far beyond its rightful position—as a servant to the heart. The ego often operates from a lower vibratory state, aligning with fear, anger, and jealously, rather than with lightness, greater understanding, and play.

Gaia: another term for planet Earth.

Heart center (energetic): composed of the energetic heart; heart chakra; low and high heart; and sacred heart.

High heart and sacred heart: parts of the heart that connect with our higher aspects.

High heart: the aspect of the heart chakra/energetic heart that connects with higher chakras, higher consciousness, and higher aspects of Self (Higher Self, Soul, Monad, etc.).

Heart, the: can refer to the physical organ, as well as the energetic center/chakra. There are multiple aspects to the heart, all of which are interconnected and affect one's function and operation both physically and energetically.

Higher aspects: the parts of the self that are connected to the Higher Self, Soul, Oversoul, Monad, Godhead, Source/Universe/God.

Higher Self: a higher conscious aspect of self that bridges the gap between the lower self and the higher aspects.

Homeostasis: our comfort zone or the balance point

at which the workings of our being are in harmony rather than stressed.

Intention: the focusing of energy for a specific outcome.

Love: Absolute Love, Divine Love, the Love of Self, the Love of God.

love: the love felt toward someone or something.

Low heart: the aspect of the heart chakra/energetic heart which aligns closely with the physical body, assists with feelings of love, generates coherence, and can feel wounded. It is the part of our heart center more closely connected with the ego personality.

Lower Self/Lower aspect: the aspect of Self that is most conscious and concerned with our current life. It comprises the ego and personality, and relates to the physical, mental, and emotional bodies.

Matrix: the misguided human narrative and experience.

Misqualified energies: energies which are incoherent, lacking integrity, and otherwise not in alignment with Love.

Monad: the totality of all things, as the individual part of the whole.

Natural Law: Physical and Spiritual Laws governed by Divine nature and Love in relationship to God/ Source/Universal energies and consciousness.

Physical heart: the physical organ responsible for pumping blood and providing life.

Positive intent: even in difficult situations, there is an opportunity for growth and healing. We are tested, sometimes intensely, through karmic agreements and situations arranged by our soul either prior to or during an incarnation. From the soul's perspective, every situation offers something to be gained.

Sacred heart: a special location within the heart space which brings peace, grace, and connects with higher aspects.

Soul trap: an energetic entanglement which forces reincarnation.

The Love That You Are: a phrase by the Spiritis Church's bishop, Glenda Green, from the Ascended Master, Jeshua (Jesus), to express the absolute, Divine Love that is at the foundation of all things.

Universal Law: Natural Law as governed by Love/God/Source/Universe.

Universal Truth: Ultimate truth as directed by Love/God/Source/Universe.

Introduction

Welcome, dear one, to a special, profound initiation. If you were not yet ready for its contents, you would not have picked up this book. Congratulations! You have come this far, living a life which offers specific and significant challenges. Confusion, pain, and suffering are common experiences for those who choose to incarnate on this planet. Because of the nature of this world, and the karma you came to experience and resolve, trials and tribulations abound. The physical realm is messy! So, what do you do when you feel a calling within your being, a growing need to release old energies and habits? With each step you take along your path, you may long to connect with and strengthen your relationship with Spirit, to bring forth a sense of security and confidence. This calling has made you curious, and it births many questions! What exceptional gifts and talents do you have? How can you know your Eternal Self and realize the grandeur of your unlimited potential? How can you meet new people, connect with different places, and learn new, unconventional ways of being? Perhaps your curiosity is leading you to peer into spaces in your psyche you have not dared to enter before . . . and you gravitate to the Language of Light, a language beyond time and space, known in its truth by your soul itself. What better way to connect with your soul than by using the language your soul speaks? Light Language, at its foundation, is a language of Love.

Love is a Divine expression of energy which creates, fuels, supports, and enhances all things in the universe. Love is free will. Love is experience. Love is truth. Love is greater understanding and connection to the Supreme, Divine, Universal Source: God-Energy. Love is the foundation of the Godhead, the Great Consciousness, wherein all souls dwell.

The Light Codes in this book can help you connect with higher understanding and concepts of Love. It can help you discover who and what we are, and can answer some of the many questions humanity has about the Great Consciousness. We wish you to know and embody the Truth of your existence, and to make contact, in your own timing, with the Godhead. The symbols presented in this book are keys that will open the locks of your being. It will be up to you and the higher aspects of your higher self and soul to know how much and how far to proceed. Trust this process. It is not a race.

This is your life, your practice, and your path. Give yourself permission to experience it fully in your own timing. Focus on your growth and development, and be open to the Beings of Love and Light to assist you and support your journey in Love.

We wish you blessings on all your discoveries yet to come. May your heart be full of wonder, openness, and curiosity.

LAARA
The Tigress of the Light,
and The Council of Light

PART I

The Masters

I have been channeling Light Language and Light Codes in multiple forms since 2016. The energies continue to move me in profound directions, and this ever-evolving process has been life-changing. As I have developed my channeling skills, I have had many spirit guides' help, including two Ascended Masters, Lady Isis, and Jeshua (Jesus), who work with me. Master Ling, a being I cherish, is my head guide. A monk from the ancient Tibetan Bön religion, he supports me in all my endeavors. I am blessed and humbled by their presence, patience, and support. I also connect with a being called "K," who is associated with Centaurian energies, and who assists me in differentiating multiple Light Language dialects. K offers wisdom from the Centaurian section of our Milky Way galaxy. In this book, when I say "we," I am referring to my Spirit Team and my *Tigress of the Light* energies, and/or the energies of the Collective Consciousness. The energies from *The Tigress of the Light* represent the accumulation of healing, wisdom, and consciousness my higher aspects wish to share with all of humanity.

The Light Codes in my books are Universal Light Codes, originating from Source, and through the Alpha Centauri star system.

To channel a Light Code (or Light Language), the first connection I make is with my own *Tigress of the Light* energies. This higher conscious aspect of myself ensures utmost honor and integrity of the energies channeled, whether it be Light Codes, Light Language, healing energies, or information. *Tigress of the Light,* along with Lady Isis, Jeshua, Master Ling, K, and other Light Beings, assist my lower incarnated aspect in connecting with Source energy, to maintain the integrity and clarity of the message throughout the entire channeling. As I connect consciously with Source energy, I bring healing, information, and wisdom down through multiple planes, dimensions, and realms, up to and including the twelfth dimensional realms, the 144-dimension expansion, or Unity Consciousness. Scientists and philosophers do not know how many dimensions, densities, and realms there are. However, in my *current humble experience*, there are twelve main dimensions, and within those twelve dimensions is a subsidiary multiple of twelve, which results in 144 dimensions. The channeled energies are brought through the various realms, timelines, and dimensions, and are focused or "actualized" into our time-space reality. As the energy I channel is ultimately Source energy, the Light Language and Light Codes I channel are available to all beings, as a pure offering of the Divine.

The Background
of Light Language

What is Light Language?

Light Language, at its foundation, is an energetic transmission of information. Its growth in worldwide popularity is because of its powerful means of assisting us with upgrading all levels of our being, clearing and cleansing our energy field and bodies, and connecting our consciousness with higher, Divine energies. When channeled correctly, Light Language is a high-vibrational, fundamental building block of the universe that can be expressed in many ways. The means by which your senses perceive energy will determine your perception of Light Language. The commonality of all expressions of Light Language is the foundation: Love. For example, people connect with Light Language in different ways, such as by:

- perceiving the energy of a physical object (living or not).
- seeing the arrangement of energy in a pattern such as sacred geometry.
- accumulating energy through Love.
- seeing patterns of light which may or may not be related to sunlight.

A Short History of Light Language

Light Language is an energetic transmission of information or healing energy which is not bound by grammar or the limitations of the human brain. It is the language of our higher aspects, our heart, and the universe. Light Language is an ancient language that humanity has known for thousands of years, since everything of the Light would be considered an expression of Light Language.

Christ's disciples channeled forms of Light Language, and Light Codes currently are shared commonly as Reiki. However, the energies Earth and humanity were engaged with prior to 2012 differ from the energies we experience now, hence we have multiple alternative forms of Reiki, and Reiki-like energies. Reiki symbols would be considered Light Codes, according to how I have come to understand Light Codes and Light Language.

New energies and healing modalities are being brought forth to assist humanity with current energies, and we can expect this download of intense energetic wisdom and information to last for another fifty to 250 years. The duration depends on humanity's response to change, and on how easily the energies of Earth can settle into a more harmonious and neutral space (the "new normal").

As previously mentioned, Light Language is an energetic transmission of information. It can be spoken, sung, signed, and expressed through sacred geometry, mathematics, and art, such as music, dance, and painting. This means that everything that is of the Light is Light Language. *Everything is energy*. All information known and unknown in the universe, as well as the universe itself, is energy. Human beings have used language to communicate information; information which, at its foundation, is energy. Our thoughts are energy. Our feelings are energy. Our knowledge, opinions, actions, and so on are all energy. However, as many of us realize, our human language is flawed. We don't have the vocabulary to describe the energetic information we connect to through meditating, deep thinking, sensing, intuition, and so on. Our language limits us, just as our brain (as amazing as it is) is limited in its ability to conceive intangible information. Unless we stretch it by conceptual thinking and learning, we find the older we get, the narrower our mind becomes. Consider, for example, humans', animals', and other critters' ability to convey information through body language or scent. There are lots of ways to communicate, but they are limited by the sender's ability to convey a message, and the receiver's ability to receive a message. Our body needs to filter and interpret information on the mental, emotional, and physical levels. For example, if someone has had a traumatic childhood that has left them feeling unsafe, they may not interpret a signal from a safe person that they are safe to be around. Until we heal enough of our wounds, our traumas and experiences color our ability to give and receive messages.

Because Light Language bypasses the limitations of our human languages and brain, it offers us a way to tap into a broader scope of information. Our filters and lenses are still in place, but the energetic transmission of Light Language can work with our limitations (and even assist us in moving past them) by healing us and raising our vibrations.

When we connect to a stream of energetic information and express it in ways such as through spoken and written means, this is called channeling. When we channel Light Language, we often bring a large block of information into our conscious and subconscious minds. We may know some of the information consciously, but some of it may remain in our subconscious minds, until it is appropriate for us to notice it. When channeled appropriately, Light Language will always work in our highest good. This is because the information is sacred, heart-connected, grounded, and channeled via our connection to our higher aspects and expanded consciousness in alignment with Love. It is the energetic language of the higher self and soul.

Light Codes and Light Language— What's the Difference?

On a fundamental level, Light Language and Light Codes are both a Divine expression of Light energy. Thus, we can use these terms interchangeably. However, there are differences between the two that are worth noting. Light Language delivers a long stream of information on a topic, with a specific message or healing. A Light Code is a condensed version of the same stream of information, with the added capability of expanding upon the topic it represents. Each Code is like a fingerprint: unique and connected to a greater picture. The Code behaves like an access point to a greater topic and serves to convey to the seeker a cache of information. It acts as a portal to an infinite amount of information.

To help you visualize this idea, consider for a moment the shape of an umbrella. Now imagine that the dome of fabric that shapes the umbrella is made of infinite space. Within that space is an unlimited amount of information on a topic. This information might be basic, or it could be complex or multidimensional. Imagine that at the tip of the umbrella's handle, there is a Light Code. Then, imagine that the shaft of the umbrella is a beam of light-energy consciousness connecting to the top of the umbrella. Our higher aspects (Higher Self, Soul, and the Monad) direct our consciousness to the information held within the expansive scope of the umbrella and connect us to the relevant information.

Whether or not you are aware of it, this is why, after working with a Light Code, you can have different responses—perhaps feeling physical sensations around your sacral chakra one day, or having vivid dreams the next day—or perhaps you notice nothing at all because your higher aspects are directing energetic information to your subconscious mind. Everyone has an individual experience with the Codes because everyone has a unique set of patterns, traumas, beliefs, talents, awareness, and sensitivity. No one's experience is better than anyone else's.

When we work with a Light Code, something magical happens. A Light Code can connect us not only to the same information Light Language channeling would provide, but it allows for the bridging and expansion of information in ways that Light Language typically doesn't. As we work with a Light Code (such as meditating on it), as we heal and grow in our consciousness and awareness and become ready for more, *the Code grows with us.*

Light Language Channeling says, "Here's an information dump. You get what you get—some is saved for later in the subconscious mind, but this is all the information. Higher self, do what you want with it." The information is elongated, offering a specific approach to receiving energy. There is room for growth, but it isn't the same as working with a Light Code. A Light Code says, "Here's some information. When you're ready for more, I will take you there." This happens because the information is succinct. It works with you to access new levels of information over time, especially as you work with it consciously.

Both Light Language and Light Codes have their purpose, and neither is better nor more useful than the other. For example, a benefit of spoken Light Language would be the related sound vibration. Some people find sound vibration to be supportive of their healing process, as it is experienced physically as well as energetically. The physical body feels sound vibrations which can help resolve energetic incoherence, disruptions, or disturbance. This powerful energetic transmission is effective for many people. Provided the Light Code has a Light Language name attached to it, Light Codes can offer sound therapy as well (like those found in this book). One can work with sound vibrations by speaking the name of the Code, especially as part of a meditation or chant.

The Benefits of Light Language and Light Codes

Light Language and Light Codes can assist us in a multitude of ways.

On a physical level, we can experience:

- better sleep,
- vivid dreams,
- increased energy,
- better digestion,
- cleansing of toxins,
- pain relief,

- healing of acute or chronic conditions,
- increased physical ability for integrating higher vibrational frequencies,
- help with physical ascension symptoms,
- and more.

On an emotional level, we can experience:

- reduced depression and anxiety,
- emotional release,
- greater levels of happiness and joy,
- a general feeling of wellness and lightness,
- more resilience in stressful situations,
- greater ability to process emotions,
- increased emotional awareness,
- and more.

On a spiritual level, we can experience:

- greater awareness and focus of our spiritual mission,
- connection to our spirit guides,
- clearing and balancing of energies,
- attunements to higher consciousness,
- alignment of the chakras,
- stronger connection to the higher self and Soul,
- upgrades in consciousness,
- grounding and integrating higher vibrational energies,
- and more.

The New Era

Changing Ages

We live in potent, turbulent times. We are in a transition of the Ages, progressing from the Piscean Age into the Aquarian Age. On an elemental level, we are moving from deep, watery Pisces into airy Aquarius... which means, on an energetic and symbolic level, that water is clashing with air. What happens when water and air mix? A lot of weather... and a lot of emotion about it all, too! The energies of water and air are both ungrounded, so we are seeing a lot of hot-headedness and fast action. We are also seeing an exponential increase in development of, and use of, technology—all of which is Aquarian.

Transitions between Ages can last up to 500 years. We are about halfway through this changeover, and are feeling the effects of Aquarius more each year. We truly are living in the Information Age! With multiple online platforms and means of sharing information, just about anything we could want to know is at our fingertips. However, this doesn't mean all information will be useful or even correct. Discernment is important, and discernment comes from knowing yourself and staying true to yourself. It is a byproduct of healing, knowledge, and standing firm in your authority.

Because we are here and involved with this time of significant change (which is challenging for most of us, since many of us aren't comfortable with change), we need tools to help us. So, we're seeing an influx of healing modalities, and more people are working with Light Language.

There is a divide in consciousness now, whereby some people are going deeper into the artificial intelligence of the AI matrix and away from the Divine, and some are choosing a path of ascension. For those of us on an ascension journey, there are tools to help us remember who we truly are. New energy modalities such as channeled Light Language bring us back to ourselves, connect us with our gifts, and enhance our talents. They teach us how to integrate energy influxes, and how to harmonize with the higher vibrational frequencies Spirit offers us.

Gaia

Our beloved planet Earth—also called Terra Blue and Gaia—is a unique planet not only within the Milky Way galaxy, but within our universe. She has consciousness, awareness, and intent, and she is a mother to all who inhabit her. She is beautiful, majestic, and powerful. The consciousness of our planet is inspiring because of her great desire to support the incarnated experience of those who seek one. She can work with a wide spectrum of energies, continuously seeking a neutral and balanced state.

The Human Body

Physical Feedback

The physical body offers an array of sensations to differentiate energies and dynamics in response to life experiences, making the body a valuable, sacred teaching tool. Physical feedback is one of the many blessings of incarnating on Gaia. For example, if you smack your head against a wall, it hurts. If you eat too many sweets, you get a tummy ache. This is *feedback*. If you enjoy stretching, and you stretch often, you are rewarded with good feelings. This is *feedback*. If you ignore angry emotions for too long, those energies manifest as physical disruptions within the body (this, too, is *feedback*). When you listen to your body and allow it to serve as a reflector for how you're feeling about life events, you can be proactive and process, release, and transmute disruptive energy that comes along. The wonderful (and challenging) thing about being human is that our body and soul record memories, events, and traumas in our physical tissues. These experiences aren't only held in our brains but are also kept in parts of our bodies (e.g., in our backs, fascia, stomachs, etc.). The soul keeps a record of all life experiences (this is how the soul learns), and the physical body is the sacred means by which the soul can experience and resolve any dysfunctional energies. If an incoherent energy isn't resolved during a lifetime, that energy is brought forward to be neutralized in the next lifetime. Whether we brought these energies in with us from the soul level, experienced a new event in this lifetime, or inherited dysfunctional energy from our parents (that can happen, too!), we can heal all of them. We are healing not only our own experiences, but our past lives, future lives, and even our ancestral and collective energies.

Our body adapts to ever-fluctuating energies. When we heal a trauma, for example, we change our energetic frequency. For example, working with the Light Codes in this book, or using techniques from Fractalline Healing™, and others, raises our baseline frequency and expands our adaptability on every level, so we can be exposed to greater physical and energetic changes with less interference to our homeostasis.

Water and Emotions

Our second chakra, the sacral center, is represented by the water element and signifies emotions. How we process energy in our emotional center and body is mirrored by our beloved planet. Consider, for example, the workings of a hurricane—hot air, cool air, water, and a lot of energy combine to create the storm system. There are enormous waves in the ocean, trees break apart, and general chaos develops. A hurricane spins, builds in intensity, and then weakens and ends. If we compare a hurricane to an emotional event within our lives, we see commonalities, usually involving a lot of hot air/wind (talking or perhaps yelling), water (tears), and energy (increased heart rate, the release of cortisol, and a disturbance in the auric field). We may even feel a spinning sensation! The difference is, how long did Gaia hold on to the storm? Hours? Perhaps a few days if it was really big? How about you? How long did you hold on to your emotional event? Some of our events, memories, and upsets haven't ever been released. That energy is still spiraling within us, causing a domino effect of triggers, upset, and energy loss. This may even be one reason you picked up this book!

The Chakra System

A (Very) Brief Explanation of
Energy and the Chakra System

Our energy moves up through our body, from our feet to our head, passing through each of the seven main chakras along the way. Imagine a masterful person (a person who is highly conscious and in full alignment with the Love That They Are) experiencing a traumatic or upsetting event. A masterful person would experience an energetic response to that upset and would move the energy up from the root chakra, through the chakra system, and ultimately release it through the crown chakra. Our masterful person would:

- encounter an event (root chakra: fire element, notice it),

- feel it (sacral center: water, emotions),

- have thoughts about it (solar plexus: air, intellect),

- transmute the energy for greater understanding (heart center: earth, change),

- use the understanding gained to express wisdoms/ thoughts (or not) (throat center: ether, expression),

- gain further sight/insight to see the situation clearly (third eye: light, sight, and insight) ... and finally,

- expand the consciousness of the event, bringing it into a neutral state (crown: iridium, spiritual connection, and awareness).

Then, the masterful person may alter their response to the situation (which may include no response). When the sacral center is drained of energy (because of a lot of emotional upset), we cannot think or see clearly. A typical person would experience energy becoming distorted, misdirected, or inhibited from moving through the system. Some of the chakra centers might not function properly or may be skipped altogether, placing a load on the remaining centers. This excess load might cause some centers to not process energy effectively, as they are designed to do. For example, if we are afraid or upset, we won't be able to connect with our third-eye chakra without distortion. This is because fear and upset prevent the third eye from functioning properly because of the energetic loss in the system (namely, at the root and sacral centers). This complex system is not the focus of this book, but it is important to have a little understanding of how the energies in our environment (or that we experience in our lives) affect our physical, mental, emotional, and spiritual function.

Exploring Healing Techniques

You may feel called to learn healing techniques, either for your own self-healing, interest, or to offer professionally. The energies of the planet and solar system are evolving and changing, both on the individual level and at the level of the human collective and beyond. If you feel called to explore different healing modalities, learn about things that inspire you—discover techniques to help you embrace your true self. Remember, that's what all of this is about—you coming back to you. No one can do it for you. But the good news is, you can do it!

Fractalline Healing™

I invite you to expand your mind and consider that in the quantum field of unlimited possibilities, there is a remarkable experience that defies our typical understanding of the 3D world. Fractalline Healing is a meditative, multi-level, multidimensional healing and self-development space you can access by altering your brainwaves and states of consciousness. Using the system offers opportunities for you to heal yourself and others, increase energy, connect with guides, set powerful intentions, and bring forward knowledge from your higher self and soul. It is a specific location with distinct features within the quantum field, accessed through a grounded, meditative state. While exploring the space and the system, healings, shifts, and downloads happen as we remain connected with our body.

Fractalline Healing was born of the need for a sacred location in the quantum realms of unlimited possibilities—one location in time and space to which everyone can bring their spiritual and healing toolkits and develop them.

I suggest you use Fractalline Healing in tandem with your work with the Light Codes. If you are a student of Fractalline Healing, you may gaze upon a Light Code prior to entering Fractalline Healing. Once you have entered, call the Light Code forward into your consciousness and work with the Code in this powerful, sacred space.

Healing Ancestral Energies

If you've done ancestral healing, it is likely you have experienced a trigger, belief, or upset for which you have offered a healing as far down your ancestral line as you could. Some lightworkers—shamans, healers, and various other metaphysical practitioners—do this type of work, but with varying success. If we address only the symptoms of an issue we've encountered (or that has been brought to our attention), and we aren't getting to the root cause of the issue actively, we aren't doing effective ancestral work. This is akin to taking a painkiller for a physical pain, but not exploring and determining the underlying cause. Of course, this can get complex quickly, depending upon how many healing, ancestral, and conscious levels one is open to, interested in, or capable of perceiving. For example, perhaps someone sprains their ankle, and takes an allopathic pain killer to mask the pain and reduce inflammation. If we look deeper, we might find that their muscles and ligaments lack strength or flexibility, increasing risk of injury. We might look at their diet and find they lack nutrients, making them prone to sprain. We might wonder, "Why are the nutrients lacking?" We'd look at their digestive system and diet and go down the rabbit hole of food sensitivities, glyphosate toxicity, and the need to incorporate organic foods into their diet. We might look at the emotional reasons the person sprained their ankle . . . Which side of the body is the injury on? What does that side represent? What chakras and meridians are involved? What was the person feeling leading up to the event? Why might they feel they can't step forward in life (since now it hurts to walk)? While we explore emotions and body symbology, we might look at their past lives, which potentially leads us to their ancestral line.

All these angles are interconnected, which is why it's important to use a holistic, multifaceted, multi-disciplinary approach. Light Codes can help us unmask and potentially heal these parts of ourselves. Although ancestral energies are not the focus of this book, you can choose to include ancestral energies in your healings and upgrades with the Light Codes and channeled messages.

Working with Light Codes

lease take your time reading and working with these symbols. While the Codes have been arranged progressively, where each builds upon the last, please use them in a sequence in which you feel guided or directed. Everyone has their own unique experience while working with Light Codes. The energies an individual needs, their sensitivity level, and their conscious or unconscious connection with the Codes will determine each user's experience. Some people feel sensations, others may "see" energies (such as perceiving shapes or lights in their mind's eye). Others may notice a different thought or memory, and some might receive nothing at all! Be the sacred witness of your own experience, remaining free of judgment, holding your intentions for the best outcome.

For most of the Light Codes in this book, at the end of each entry, I have provided a starting point for your work through a practice or meditation. However, there are many ways Light Codes can be incorporated into your life. You may think of them as energy generators, radiating a loving frequency into your environment. The subtle body absorbs this information and sends it to your higher aspects to be integrated and worked with further. I've seen them used in ceremony, art creation, on clothes, placed on walls during construction, pinned on the refrigerator for the whole family to see, and so on. You may charge your crystals, food, supplements, or water with Light Codes. These Codes are wonderful for personal and professional healing, and can be used every day, or reserved for sacred ceremonies. Use Light Codes with your pets as well, by placing a Light Code close to them or charging their food or water with a Light Code. The sky's the limit!

Meditating

As a baseline practice for working with Light Codes, use the Grounding Practice Meditation provided to help you become present, grounded, relaxed, and open to receive the messages and energies on a conscious level. If your favorite meditations bring you into a grounded state, use those instead. As with all things, the more conscious we are, the more connected and empowered we are, and the more meditation expands our conscious mind and helps us tap into the collective unconscious. That said, Light Codes work with us for our highest good, whether or not we are aware of them.

Grounding Practice Meditation

Sit in a chair with your feet flat on the floor. Relax. Breathe. On each inhale, imagine your feet are suction cups, pulling energy up from the earth. On each exhale, relax. With each inhale, imagine your feet drawing energy up from Gaia, through the floor, into your legs. Feel the energy moving up in your body with each in-breath until it reaches the top of your head. Release it out of the top of your head (through your crown chakra). Imagine the energy flowing up and out like water cascading from a fountain. Practice this grounding exercise often, so it becomes second nature. Using this process at the beginning of your meditation practice will help center you and prepare you to enter any level of awareness you may wish to access. Grounding connects your heart and mind. It can promote wellness, improve sleep, lower your blood pressure, and reduce stress and anxiety. It's a great way to start and end each day!

Six Direction Meditation

If you would like to work with the Light Codes and their accompanying messages from a deeper meditative state, try the Six Direction Meditation. This meditation builds on the Grounding Practice to bring your attention to all six directions of your energy body (your aura). Engaging in this meditation helps you achieve an "expansive state" whereby you are still grounded and present within your body, but you are more in tune with the energies within and around you.

Six Direction Meditation Instructions

Once you feel the energy of the earth flowing up from the bottoms of your feet into your body and out the top of your head, direct your awareness to your back. Feel into the space behind you, about an arm's length in distance, while continuing to pull energy from the earth into your feet and out the top of your head. Maintain a connection with your back and bring your attention to the sides of your body. Feel about an arm's length in distance into the space around your side-body. Continue pulling energy into your feet and out the top of your head. Then, bring your attention to your front-body while maintaining the connection with your back and sides, feeling an arm's length into the space in front of you. Next, bring your attention to your feet, allowing yourself to feel into the ground again, to a depth of about an arm's length. While pulling energy into your feet and out the top of your head, bring your attention to the space above your head, about three feet above you. Now, feel the space behind you, beside you, in front of you, deep into the earth, and above your head simultaneously. Continue to bring energy up from the earth into your feet, and out the top of your head. When you are ready, bring your attention back to your feet and to the energy flowing through your body. Open your eyes.

This is a wonderful meditation to prepare you for working with any of the symbols in this book. Do this meditation, then open your eyes and look at the symbol. You will be open and able to receive the healings, messages, upgrades, and frequencies necessary for you.

General Meditation for Working with Light Codes

To enhance your experience, prior to doing this General Meditation, do the Grounding Practice and the Six Direction Meditation.

Sit quietly and comfortably in a place you won't be disturbed. Close your eyes and quiet your mind. With every slow, deep breath you take, feel yourself sinking into the ground. When you are ready, open your eyes and gaze upon the Code. Feel its energy. Try to remain open to the various ways the Light Code can speak to you. You may feel sensations or perceive light, or thoughts may pop into your mind. Stay with the Light Code for as long as is comfortable. When you are done, thank the Code for its help. Use this symbol as often as you feel is right for you.

Working with the Messages and Light Codes

Although these messages are channeled from Universal Source, we are each limited by our personal language and our individual history. Therefore, as you read, meditate upon, and contemplate the messages and stories, apply your own interpretation. Allow your own truth to emerge. Ponder your own life story. How has your life been shaped, directed, or defined by the wounds of your soul and the beauty you've experienced? For any Code, story, or message, consider multiple viewpoints—what do they each mean in the context of who you are and who you want to become?

Fire Safety

Several times in this book, we suggest you work with a tea light candle. Please practice good, common sense fire safety while working with a flame. Have a bowl of water close by, use a solid, safe candle holder, ensure there is ample clearance for the flame, and never leave a candle unattended. If you feel you would like to enter a deeper meditation and possibly fall asleep, please extinguish the flame, or have the candle in a bathtub with no fire hazards nearby. If you'd like to place a candle on top of a Light Code, please do not use the image in the open book. Prior to placing a candle on top of a Code, trace the Light Code on a separate piece of paper, and place the candle on the traced image.

A Note to
the Reader

Although you may choose to read the Light Codes out of order, I recommend that the first time you read through them in the order presented, working with each symbol sequentially. The energies within this book are cumulative and work with us as individuals to prepare us for the next consecutive symbol, all the way to the finale of the Godhead. It is, however, your choice.

When I write "we," such as "We invite you to...," the "We" I am referring to is the collective energies of Jeshua (Jesus), Lady Isis, K, Master Ling, and the author of this book, in association with *The Tigress of the Light*, or "the collective consciousness." You can use the message associated with the Light Code to assist you in deciding the most appropriate meditation or other use (such as charging tea with the symbol and having a ceremony) for each Code.

Although this is a channeled work, it's important to recognize those who have played an instrumental role in my spiritual development. Even when channeling, we draw upon what we have learned, which is why it's important to have an open mind and continue to learn from those with whom we resonate. I am blessed to have teachers in my life who support and encourage me. Rosalyn L. Bruyere and

Ken Weintrub are a significant part of my foundation, and you will find some of their teachings throughout this book.

There may be segments in this book you find confusing, with expansive concepts and language that may be difficult to understand initially. If you find a passage challenging, regard each word individually. For example, Adamantine particles "are the interconnection between divine rhythms." This sentence may seem senseless, but we urge you to tune in to your feelings as you consider each word. What does *interconnection* mean to you? What does *divine rhythm* mean to you? How do these words relate to one another? Can you stop the intellectual dissection of the words and interpret them with your emotions? If you cannot make sense of a passage, simply continue working with the Light Code and what *is* clear to you. When you revisit the notion at a future time, you will see it in a different light. Often, the spaces and energies we explore in this book are nuanced and complex. They are multidimensional and multifaceted, and within each facet and dimension there are octaves of energies. Sometimes we explore concepts that may seem similar to concepts already covered—so similar you might regard them as being the same. However, with the help of the Light Codes, we can discern the slight variation in the energies that separate one concept from the other. Finally, you may notice that not all the information we share aligns with current world thinking. We invite you to read and experience this book with your sense of the Eternal Self; with the Love That You Are.

Enjoy!

LAARA

PART II

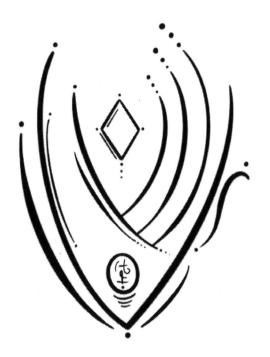

Tomohiya

(To-mo-hi-ya)

SACRED CONNECTION

*Connect to your infinite, particle-like nature
and set the stage for the journey ahead.*

Your journey begins by gaining a greater understanding of your sacred connection to Source. This connection exists among all things, in all dimensions, and it goes beyond the limitations of time. Your sacred connection is the union of the Great Love—Love in its truest, purest sense. While we understand "love" (with a lower-case "*l*") is a feeling we have about someone or something, this Light Code, Tomohiya, allows you to deepen your experience of greater, Universal Love (with a capital "*L*").

Imagine you are a tiny particle of energy floating in a vast, warm, protected space. This space is larger than anything you can imagine, but instead of feeling fearful, you feel supported and comfortable. This sacred space of Universal Love provides a means to begin your journey into deeper, expansive realms of consciousness. You are a spark of Light comprising Love and infinite possibility. As a particle, you can be anything, connect with any consciousness, and dance with (and in) many energy streams. You can morph into any color, pattern, or shape, and vibrate and resonate with any sound . . . your potential is *unlimited!*

$\backsim$

If you feel this is a complex concept (and is a lot to take in), meditate on this Light Code using the meditation below. Check in with this notion later (perhaps once you have finished this book) and compare how you are now with how much you have grown *after* you complete the practices in this book. For now, meditate upon Tomohiya with the meditations provided at the beginning of this book, or with the meditations below.

If you already resonate with this Light Code's message, soften your mind. Allow your consciousness to expand. Perhaps you will discover more layers, shapes, patterns, or energetic connections of yourself and beyond with this thought exercise. Maybe you can tune in to a kaleidoscope of colors and geometric patterns. There is no right or wrong, and there is no end goal. We are inviting you to claim this energy—the energy of all that is and all that can be—and assisting you in connecting with all things sacred.

As you engage with this Light Code, invite in the direction and guidance of your higher aspects, the Beings of Love and Light who support you, and the Great Spirit (God, Source, Universe, or another term you prefer). You have embarked on a journey in which you will step, one foot at a time, into the Sacred. Your curiosity may inspire you, but your heart leads the way. The ego stays behind, minding the tasks of living in a human body with a personality . . . it does not follow you to the places you will go. By meditating on this Light Code, you connect to your infinite, particle-like nature, and set the stage for the journey ahead. It's time to step farther into your ascension process.

Meditation

Part 1

Get comfortable. Slow and deepen your breath. Let go of the thoughts of the day, what you've been doing, and what you have ahead of you. Be present with your breath. Take this moment for yourself. There is no rush. Work with the grounding meditation at the beginning of this book. When you are ready, gaze at the Light Code. Breathe as though you are inhaling the energies the Code emits. Do this for as long as you need to before progressing to Part 2 of this exercise.

Part 2

Declare, "I am ready, willing, and able to walk a sacred path." Ask your divine guidance to be ever-present with you. Declare, "I choose to connect with myself as the sovereign, divine, Being of Light that I am." Say, "I choose to remain in perfect alignment with the process and move in unison with divine timing."

Breathe.

Next, while gazing upon the symbol, imagine yourself as a beautiful particle of Light. Breathe as this particle, dance and move as this particle, and be open to receiving whatever information, on any level, Tomohiya offers you. When you are complete, express your gratitude to the energies, Beings of Light, and yourself for being here.

Kalukala

(Ka-loo-ka-la)

GROUNDED AND PRESENT

To be grounded and present is to focus our energy consciously on a single point in time and space.

What does it mean to be grounded and present? For some people, it means to bring energy from the universe in through the crown chakra. For others, it might mean to bring earth energy into the body from the chakras at the bottom of the feet. While these methods are both good practices, they aren't complete in themselves. To be truly grounded and present is to focus your energy on a single point in time and space, while remaining connected to the earth and our heart space. Over the years, we have seen human beings using strong focus to do remarkable things, like bending metal spoons, or manifesting a solid object in their hands. When we have this level of command of presence, focus, and energy, we are truly grounded, present, and in harmony with the world.

It is possible to focus our energy to this degree, but it takes time, effort, discipline, and patience. Some of us might find ourselves there one day, but on our journey of self-mastery, we do not need to bend metal spoons. What *is* essential to our path of self-mastery is building our Love.

We can build our Love by taking time every day to tune in to our heart space, embracing heart-felt feelings such as gratitude or joy, and focusing on these feelings while we engage with Light Codes. As we deepen our focus on The Love That We Are, eventually we can contact the particles that respond to the commands of our Love: adamantine particles.

We encourage you to include building your Love and connecting to adamantine particles as part of your grounding practices. You may bring Universal energy in through your crown chakra, down your body, and out your root chakra, or down your legs and out your feet. Inhale the energy, and on the exhale, release the energy into the earth. Or, you may prefer to breathe the energy in through the bottoms of your feet, and on the exhale, release it out of your crown, as suggested in this book. Either method is acceptable. We want to move the energy through the body in a cyclical pattern, which will build the toroidal energy field around your body. As you practice this, inhaling energy in and exhaling energy out, you may notice momentum building as the energy cycles through your body. This takes practice, so if you don't feel it immediately, this is normal. Doing this exercise will help to release energetic blocks and stagnation in your body as well as bring balance to your nervous system, among other things.

Once you have established energetic momentum, gaze upon Kalukala. The purpose of the Code is to assist you in gathering and building more energy in your being while deepening your connection to your adamantine particles. As you direct your gaze on the Code, feel the momentum increasing. When you are ready, ask the Code to assist you in developing and strengthening your connection to your adamantine particles. Stay relaxed. Breathe and cycle the energy.

Note: On a different day (or even as part of the exercise today), try cycling the energy through your body in the opposite direction of your preference. It's helpful to mix up the directions, so you remain balanced, and so you do not develop unnecessary rigidity or a false belief that one way is better than the other. Consider this ambidextrous breathwork!

Haliqima

(Ha-lee-kee-ma)
EXPANDING AWARENESS

*Choosing a life of expanding awareness
is continual, omnipresent, and
never to be finished or completed.*

To some extent, every choice we make in life matters. Free will determines many aspects of our life, namely which paths we choose and with which distractions we engage. Along the way, sometimes fueled by karmic contracts, we receive lessons and experiences through events which are predetermined by the soul.

The free will choices we make throughout our life (including pre-birth and childhood), as well as our thought patterns and the personality traits we try on, all can determine how smoothly we walk the path of life. Eventually, we find ourselves at a crossroads. We must choose either to continue living life as we know it (perhaps remaining in a limited, habitual way of being) or to expand and move into a multifaceted, multidimensional lifestyle.

This Light Code is imparting wisdom about this crossroads now. You can remain as you are, continuing along your life's path, or you can take a leap of faith and step into the ever-expanding energies of consciousness.

Expanding our consciousness and levels of awareness assists with the healing and release of many limiting programs and beliefs contained within the lower self. Our ability to move harmoniously through life and integrate more information through a broader lens is strengthened. Often, our traumas and triggers color our abilities to see clearly, and they prevent us from behaving in accordance with our Love. Our increased perception can encourage and support us to heal our wounds while simultaneously broadening our ability to embrace life from multiple angles and to view it from multiple vantage points.

With expanded awareness, we judge ourselves less, thereby deepening our self-realization and healing. We notice and release low-vibrational thoughts and reactions easily, so there is more room for kindness, patience, acceptance, gratitude, and Love—for ourselves and others. Relationships in all areas of our life heal, and we make deeper connections with people and nature. Our experience of the world becomes positive, rather than a struggle or something to be feared, shamed, or avoided.

We magnify the connections with our higher self and soul as we continue to expand our consciousness and heal our hearts. As our heart heals and expands, so does our consciousness and awareness. Our heart loves to grow and expand, touching more beautiful hearts and their higher aspects.

Our higher self and soul, although already wise and interconnected, are also seeking greater awareness, understanding, and experience. They want to grow in all ways. The pattern of healing and expansion becomes cyclical, each step bringing about greater levels of harmony and consciousness.

There is no limit to how far your awareness can take you. This Light Code offers to assist you in expanding your consciousness and awareness. If you do not understand its energy or message, try not to limit its potency or restrict its offering. Welcome the energies this Code offers and work with it. There is nothing to fear. All Light Codes work in infinite ways as your higher aspects and Love direct.

Use the meditation at the beginning of this book to ground yourself. Be present, quiet, and still. When you are ready, open your eyes and gaze upon the Code. Breathe in its energies, sensing it. Declare in your own words that you choose to continue expanding your consciousness and awareness in alignment with Love.

When you are finished, offer thanks to the Light Code and to any Light Beings who assisted you.

Kumara'aha

(Koo-ma-ra, aha)

EMBODIMENT OF INFINITE POTENTIAL

Ascension is only possible if we relinquish our fear of Truth and the vast scale of the self and the Universe.

Energy is always in a state of infinite potential. Since everything is energy, when we refer to the Infinite, we are acknowledging everything that is, was, and *ever could be*. Humans are Eternal Beings of the Light, an incarnated form of infinite potential. With enough focused energy and consciousness, we can create or do *anything*.

As eternal beings of the Light, human beings have the capacity through our expanded consciousness and awareness to embody infinite potential. After all, everything is in a state of potentiality until consciousness focuses on it, turning what is *potential* into what is *actual*! This natural Law is, in fact, how a being becomes incarnated. The soul desires to experience life in a physical body, so it focuses its energy and consciousness on a particular point in time and space. The result: physical life. Part of our soul's awakening and ascension journey in the physical body includes releasing all limiting factors—thoughts, beliefs, and energies—that inhibit our relationship with infinite potential.

Embracing infinite potential will allow your being to carry more energy, increasing its ability to integrate a larger range of frequencies. Increasing our energetic frequency range assists with oversensitivity symptoms such as overwhelm, anxiety, and fear. Our ability to carry more energy relates directly to how functionally sensitive we are to our environment. We want to be sensitive in a positive way, and be able to use information, rather than resist or shy away from what our senses naturally perceive. Our goal is to work masterfully with information in all the ways we can know it, such as through sight, smell, taste, hearing, knowing, etc. This information will help us flow in oneness with the universe. These are just some of the many benefits of embodying infinite potential—they are as infinite as the potential outcomes themselves!

Kumara'aha shows us where we hold fears or other limitations which restrict our conscious awareness of our multidimensional and multifaceted self. This Code offers two primary energies. It helps release our fears of infinite potential, and it assists us in expanding our consciousness to include infinite potential and all that means. If we don't know our limitations, we can ask this Code during meditation, "Where are the limitations within my being?" These limitations can be found at any level, in any dimension, in any aspect of life, and on any plane—in our mental, emotional, physical, or spiritual bodies. Therefore, it's important to ask our spirit guides, higher aspects, and the Light Code to show us where we are (unintentionally) limiting ourselves.

The second stage of working with this symbol is to embrace the expansion of your conscious awareness. After you have unearthed a limitation, if you feel ready to expand, you may do both exercises below back to back. Make sure enough time is given to discovering and releasing your limitation(s) before moving on to the second part. Multiple limitations can be revealed throughout your expansion process, which is often an ongoing part of life.

Meditation

Part 1

Once you feel relaxed, grounded, and connected with your heart space, ask your guides and Kumara'aha to bring your attention to a limited aspect of your being. Remain soft and relaxed. This demeanor will afford you the best connection to messages from Spirit and the Code. Once you have realized a limitation (such as through a vision, sensation, thought, memory, knowing, sound, smell, taste, feeling, or in some other way), breathe with it. Practice relaxing around what is being brought to your awareness. Ask questions to help you release or resolve the limitation. You may need to forgive or offer compassion or Love. Do whatever is needed, asking the Code to help you. Once you have sat with the thoughts, feelings, etc. for a period that feels right, you may feel a lightness or an increase of energy, or you may yawn or experience another form of confirmation that an energy has been released. Now, if you are ready, conclude the meditation, or request that another limitation be shown to you. Or you may choose to move into the second part of this process: *expansion.*

Part 2

Still in your meditative state, ask Kumara'aha and your guides to assist you in expanding your conscious awareness. Deepen your breath. As you inhale, roll your eyes upward toward your third eye and *feel* your energy body expanding. Don't *force* it. Remain quiet, relaxed, and receptive. Breathing deeply, guide your energy outward to fill the room you're sitting in. With your breath, grow your energy body even bigger, filling your house. Once you've filled your house, fill your community, your city, country, and eventually, the planet. Once you have expanded your energy to include Gaia, ask the symbol again to help you connect with infinite potential. Breathe here for as long as it feels appropriate. When you are ready, bring your attention back to Gaia, then your country, your city, your community, your house, and the room you're sitting in. Focus your breath back on your body, pulling earth energy up through the bottom of your feet until you are ready to open your eyes. Offer gratitude to the Light Code and your spirit guides for their help.

Takahanama

(Ta-ka-ha-na-ma)

I AM THE ONE

*Nothing will strengthen you
more than standing with yourself.*

This Light Code holds the unique, sacred key to deepen your authentic soul connection. With the connection comes the opportunity for further healing, and the potential to remember past teachings so you can walk through this lifetime with clarity, support, and wisdom.

Humanity's individual and collective consciousness, connected to the Great Consciousness of the Great Spirit of the universe, is amplifying. As we embrace our true nature, our thoughts, wishes, desires, and actions carry more weight. The quality of our manifestations also improves, and we may notice more synchronicities, bolstering our confidence in our ability to regain and strengthen our sacred self. Our Light channel (the focused energy and consciousness of our higher aspects to our physical body) is strengthening, especially as we choose to release all that no longer serves us and seek self-mastery. This Code offers a myriad of Light channel upgrades, so a greater range of energy can be moved both from the soul to the body, and from the body to the soul. These upgrades can also assist us in further clearing and cleansing lower vibrational energies.

Takahanama shows you the importance of your presence on Gaia. It serves as a reminder that humanity and the collective at large need and want your energy, gifts, and talents. Sometimes you may doubt this truth or question your spiritual path. If you face doubts, sit with this symbol. Nothing is stronger than your own presence and energy. This is where many people go astray... they forget to be present with their own self, their own energy. Nothing outside of you is stronger than *you*. Nothing offers you confidence, power, or wisdom more than you do.

There is no other being exactly like you. You are the One. Once you know, understand, and embody this truth, you will be so full of your Light and Love, you will cease to know their opposites. You will be abundant, and a guide for others to follow. However, remember that as we embody new frequencies, we alter our relationship with our ego. There is no room for the ego where we are going. However, we must offer all levels of our being (including our lower aspects) the time, patience, and Love they deserve. There is no rush or race. We can take as many lifetimes as we need to embody the truths spoken throughout this book. The more pressure, resistance, or upset we create, the longer it will take. Simple, isn't it? So, be kind to yourself, and your evolution will go smoothly.

You have come so far on your journey of self-discovery and remembering your true empowered self. "Takahanama"

reflects your divine energy. Meditate with this Code for several minutes, repeating to yourself, "I am the One." When you feel ready, perform the ceremony below.

You may also use this symbol as part of a New Moon ceremony, or as part of your birthday ceremony. Create a special altar—something new you haven't built before. You don't need to bring in new items... you can rearrange or swap out objects such as crystals, candle holders, or feathers. Place a candle in the center of your altar. You may find it helpful to trace this Light Code onto a piece of paper. Place the Code propped up behind the candle so it's upright, facing you. (Have a small bowl of water handy for safety when lighting candles, and keep the book or paper with the symbol a safe distance from the candle flame. Practice practical, safe fire sense.) Create a circle with your favorite objects, such as flowers, leaves, or crystals. If you like to smudge, do so now.

When you are ready, in your own words, offer gratitude for this opportunity. Next, ask this symbol and Spirit for help. State your intention or make your request. Light the candle. Meditate for a few minutes, gazing upon the Light Code and holding your requests in your mind while allowing more details to reveal themselves. When you are finished, bow your head and heart to your altar. So be it. Allow the candle to burn down.

Holoku

(Ho-lo-ku)

SACRED FIRE

Working with the sacred fire is akin to
working in harmony with yourself,
because the sacred fire represents the
I AM Presence: your True, Divine Self.

From time to time, you may find it helpful to work with sacred fire. This is a holy fire, representing qualities like Truth, balance, harmony, and the release of energies that impede your consciousness from operating from its natural, authentic place. Used by Ascended Masters and those seeking higher levels of conscious alignment, you can invoke the Sacred to bring about any of these qualities, as well as to release misqualified energies and lack of Love. It's useful to contemplate areas that you may need to rebalance—including previous lifetimes, timelines, ancestral energies, contracts (of both the "real world" and energetic agreements and entanglements), and karmic relationships. The sacred fire supports the balance of the elemental kingdoms of Gaia, earth, air, fire, water, and ether. We can use the sacred fire to enhance our connection to and use of these important elements, whether in our day-to-day life, or in a ceremonial manner. The sacred fire also assists with creation and transformation. When we call upon the energies of the sacred fire to help us, it is wise to remember that this energy is holy and should be used for truthful purposes only, for harmonizing, or for bringing about peace to yourself or to a situation. Working with the sacred fire is akin to working in harmony with yourself, because the sacred fire represents the I AM Presence: your true, divine self. We may consider offering the sacred fire Love, as a way of offering Love to ourselves.

Holoku represents the sacred fire, offering all the purposes, qualities, and power carried by the sacred fire. Meditate upon this Light Code and connect to the sacred fire as a way of clearing your mind, energy field, and body, especially if you are an empath or have racing thoughts. You can use this Code as part of a candle ceremony to symbolize and invoke sacred fire energies and presence. Draw this Code on a special piece of paper and then place a lit tea light on top of your drawing. You may also use the sacred fire to assist you energetically to burn away any misqualified energies, lack of Love, lower vibrational thoughts/beliefs, and anything that no longer serves your highest purpose. When you complete your time with Holoku and the sacred fire, to close the ceremony, offer your gratitude.

Akumaha

(A-ku-ma-ha)

RELEASE RESTRICTIONS

By allowing others to live their life
according to their free will and destiny, we
can observe freedom within ourselves.

From the depths of our being comes a knowing as old as the Eternal Self. Your soul, since the dawn of its existence, has embodied and radiated a profound, fundamental knowing of freedom and Love of the most pure and high. Freedom and Love are Truths of your Self. Anything that is contrary or serves to suppress or alter your self's Truth is a program superimposed upon your being. Humanity carries these programs for a variety of reasons, but they do not reflect our fundamental Truth. The heart feels the weight of these false beliefs and programs, suppressing our Love and distorting our reality, perpetuating an inaccurate sense of self. The suppression of our Love disconnects us from Source, which induces energetic and emotional upset within our lower aspects. This can lead us to inflict our feelings and beliefs upon another person, unintentionally continuing the cycle of suppression and restriction of Love.

Our Love is made free by offering freedom to others. By supporting others to live their life according to their Love, free will, and destiny, we support ourselves in our freedom and Love. This can feel challenging for a variety of reasons, many of which are connected to our culture, our ancestors, and our life experiences, and reflect the many false programs and beliefs to which we have subscribed. For example, we might not want our children to stray far from our home town because we believe home is where they will be safe. This desire may stem from a belief that there is something in the world that we ourselves find frightening. However, restrictions are felt far deeper than whether we feel we have the choice to stay in a city or move away from family. Our choices can feel restricted by our own internal fears, or external forces such as from family members or other persons of influence. These limiting energies can impact whether we feel we can choose our own career, partner, friends, even the clothes we wear or the food we eat.

This Light Code offers healing to any areas in our life in which we feel constricted, whether it be initiated from internal or external circumstances. However, we can move deeper, and discover more about the pivotal limiting energies and the effect they have in our spiritual life. Since our outer world mirrors our inner world, when we have restrictions in our outward life, we hold significant energetic restrictions within our being. If we are to be truly free of all energies (including false or limiting programs or beliefs), we must first acknowledge that we have *accepted* restrictions. This acceptance helps us reclaim our power and determine for ourselves that we are not a powerless victim, but that, in fact, the opposite is true. As beings of incredible power and intelligence, we are choosing (for a period) the *experience* of the illusion of a lack of freedom and restraint. Since our life is lived on the 3D plane, there are laws that govern this realm—not as an act of limitation, but as an act of experience. This Code can help us work on many levels and layers of restraint, including those of the physical world, ancestral and family lines, false and limiting beliefs, and those we may impose on another person, further imprisoning us in a suppressive pattern.

There are many options for you to work with as you engage with this Light Code. You may work on a large scale, inclusive of many levels, such as those mentioned above, or you may enjoy working on whatever topic you feel is predominant in your life. Be clear on the energies with which you are working. Before engaging with the Light Code, consider what your life would look like without these restrictions. Hold in your mind an image of a positive outcome, not only for yourself, but for the grand effect this healing can have on your family, your ancestral line, and all of humanity. You don't need to release all restrictions at once, but there is nothing to say you can't! However, it may be wise to work with one level at a time and ask the consciousness of the Light Code to assist you in healing and clearing fully and completely.

Meditate on Akumaha with your topic. Sit with the presence and consciousness of the Code and allow it to share its incredible healing potential. When you are finished, offer gratitude to the Light Code and the Beings of Light who love and assist you.

Tularuma

(Too-la-roo-ma)

RELEASE THE PAST

*To move into our most divine and truthful
expression, we must release our past.*

On its surface, releasing the past may seem daunting and complex, for there are many layers, levels, and emotions to consider. However, you can dwell in old energies, or you can choose to leave them behind. You have free will. It is your *choice*.

When you choose to release the past, we, the Beings of Light who support you, along with this Light Code, offer energies that will help you move into a new paradigm, a new way of being. To do this, you let go of your old programming, false beliefs, habits, and perhaps even parts of your lifestyle. You can complicate things by dissecting your ancestral lines, your karma, your past lives, and all the horrible trauma and illness you have endured *ad infinitum*. You can feel every inch of your pain and suffering, and even feel virtuous while wallowing in it!

Truthfully, if human beings didn't carry these old energy patterns, triggers, and traumas lifetime after lifetime, the dysfunctional energies would have been released long ago, and this planet would be a utopia! However, humanity is consumed by two great deceptions—the false virtue of pain and suffering, and the fear of our unlimited, powerful potential. It's important to note that this message is not one of judgment, shame, or blame. These actions belong with pain and suffering, and are not part of Love, nor are they imbued with the sentiment Tularuma carries.

Every person who subscribes to the deception of pain and suffering finds value (on some level) in not claiming their rightful power. For example, someone who is chronically ill finds something of benefit while in a sickly state. We could say the same thing about someone who enters dysfunctional relationships, whether in their personal life or professional life. Regardless of the many ways that one may struggle with relationships (whether the relationship is with one's health, or with a person, place, or thing), one entertains the challenging dynamic and chooses, for whatever reason, a relationship that leads to pain and suffering. We understand that this is a frustrating and triggering truth, which is why it's important to gain clarity on this topic.

Human beings are so powerful that we can leave behind all forms of dysfunction, illness, upset, traumas, imbalances, and energies that aren't aligned with Divine truth. We can rise above these concepts, patterns, and programs—even ones that have been carried for lifetimes or generations. Nothing prevents their release when a person makes a clear decision, and then, aligned with this decision, focuses their energy and follows through with action.

We realize, dear one, that you may not be ready to believe that all pain and suffering can be released in a holy minute. *That is okay.* We realize you may not be ready to reclaim this level of empowerment or change enough of yourself for an obvious result to manifest. Life can be extremely complicated, and it's often challenging to know the best course of action to heal any one issue. Your life experience is governed by free will, and your choices are supported by universal Laws, and the Beings of Love and Light who support you. We feel it is time for you, as a beloved Being of the Light, to know the truth of your power to transmute pain and suffering. We know and understand the confusion and perceived lack of support felt and experienced by so many on this planet. It is a big test to navigate the density of the 3D world—it takes energy to change energy.

The reality of the 3D world is that of sensation. Even in transcending pain and suffering, you will still feel the physical feedback of this realm. However, you can move into a state of consciousness where you hold more mastery over your experiences and those experiences remain in balance with your Love. This means, when you experience an illness or dysfunctional event, it will hold greater *meaning* for you. You will be in tune with your higher aspects, and potentially empowered by the experience, rather than feeling victimized or defeated by it. As you grow stronger in your alignment with Love, you may even experience less intense dysfunction, as your energy flows more freely within and around you.

When you feel ready to move toward leaving pain and suffering as you know it as a thing of the past, this Light Code will wait for you, with many divine Beings of Love and Light to support you. You may start small, picking away at triggers and thought patterns you know are false and that perpetuate pain and suffering. If you have never moved into clarity or a new way of being (a life with minimal pain and suffering), we invite you to do so. Write affirmations to support yourself in this process.

Some examples to use are:

- "I choose to release fully all energies that distort the full expression of my Love."

- "I choose to step into my truthful state of being."

- "It is my free will to release all past, present, and future relationships with false programs and beliefs."

- "I choose to move into my rightful, divine expression of pure, unobstructed Loving consciousness."

- "I am now claiming my full divine, Loving energy."

Working with Tularuma brings forth a special spirit team whose task it is to assist people in the transition from living out of truth, back into truth.

We invite you to sit with the Code and your affirmations in front of you. Take a moment. Allow yourself to become grounded and present. Focus your mind and energy on this meditative process. You can shift your entire consciousness into a different state of being.

When you are relaxed and focused, gaze upon the Code. Breathe deeply for a few moments. Say your affirmations out loud. Feel, as deeply as possible, what these affirmations mean for you. Feel their depth. Feel how profoundly life-changing they are. Feel them work with the energies of the Light Code, and how they all interact with your energy. Breathe. Remain focused on releasing all past energies.

Continue to move more deeply into the truth of who you are. Once this process feels complete, thank the Code, the Beings of Light who support you, and yourself. You may return to this Light Code at any time you feel yourself engaging with false or disempowered energies.

Lamahti

(La-mah-ti)

INNOCENCE, "BABY CHI"

Love is innocent.

Dear one, at your core, you are as innocent as a beautiful new blade of grass. We, as Spirit, do not judge any false notions within your existence. We only observe and enfold you as your most natural state of Love. Love is innocent. Innocence is a sweet purity of divine nature. Innocence is your true, core nature, void of misqualified energies, programs, false beliefs, or karmic entanglements. We wish for you to begin or to embrace more deeply this truth of who you are. By doing so, you open yourself up to deeper, more profound connections, not only within yourself, but with others as well. As you call forward and tune in to your innate innocence, you invite in others' sweetness and gentleness, and you ask the authentic nature of Love to greet you. Love meets Love. Love reflects Love.

We wish to clarify that "innocent" in the context of this message does not mean weak or vulnerable, as innocence is often associated with babies who cannot care for themselves. However, in the superlative sense of "innocent," its meaning is opposite to a baby's vulnerability and defence-lessness. Innocent means standing in the power of Divine Light, unaffected by the confusion of low-vibrational ener-gies. Innocence is strong in its conviction, holding firm in all that is true in the highest form. It is an ego-less position, with full connection and embodiment of the I AM. Babies come into this world with some of this divine connection intact, and we as adults recognize this as innocence. We want to nurture and preserve the innocence we perceive because our heart doesn't want this little being to lose con-tact (however temporarily) with their true divine nature. Babies remind us of what we have forgotten and help us connect with eternal energies once again.

Baby chi (baby energy) is fresh, life energy. This baby, innocent chi offers all the energy necessary to grow and nourish a physical body and take in the enormous world of information the soul wants to gather. If one doesn't pos-sess the consciousness to connect to Source energy another way, baby chi is as close as one can be to Source energy in a physical body until it is time to cross over. Therefore, the Light Code Lamahti, which addresses this topic, is important. It helps you to tune in to innocence, bringing you closer to Source energy with the wonder, awe, and sweetness of baby chi.

We invite you to remember what it's like to be around a baby human being, animal, or plant. Choose whichever of these calls forward your heart, and triggers the stron-gest feelings of Love, gentleness, or perhaps your "it's so cute!" emotions, and imagine it in your heart and mind's eye. Remember what this feels like. Deepen your breath and close your eyes, feeling into the emotions and sensations your thought brings. When you are ready, open your eyes and gaze at the symbol. Breathe deeply, allowing the symbol to offer you its energy. Energetically and emotionally, follow the symbol to where it wants to take you. If emotions arise, allow them to come up, then allow them to pass. Remain in the flow. When you are ready, ask the Code to assist you in connecting to your innocence. Once you have reached as far as you can go, ask the Code to help you anchor this truth within your being. Breathe. When you feel complete, thank the Code and Spirit for their help.

Tukhmanaha

(Too-kah-ma-na-ha)

CONNECTING WITH
UNCONSCIOUS ENERGIES

*One paradox of being human is that
we don't know what we don't know.*

Every day brings a new opportunity for self-discovery, to be enjoyed by our lower and higher selves and soul. We are on a journey to learn about ourselves and what it means to be living in this body. During our lifetimes, we come to learn a range of aspects about ourselves, yet there are still parts of us that remain a mystery. These mysterious parts can be connected to any or all potential levels of the mental, emotional, physical, and spiritual bodies.

The path of self-discovery offers many opportunities and challenges. Those seeking to live a balanced, fruitful life learn that there are many entanglements (energies, beliefs, concepts, or patterns) that need to be acknowledged, healed, and released. These entanglements can be rooted in personal or ancestral family lessons, or in personal or collective karma, to name a few. Entanglements that cause distress aren't always what they seem, adding to the mystery of being human. Our soul, for example, often engages with tough lessons that are an opportunity to learn and advance. Typically, these challenges are in alignment with Love, even if the lower self finds the energy harsh. We can also learn lessons our soul directs that showcase where we are lacking Love or are out of harmony with Love. We can refer to these as "shadow energies," and can include unhealthy habits or life choices that do not support a happy, abundant, Love-filled life. By releasing our shadow aspects, we can reclaim our Love, power, authority, and connection to the divine from the lower self, all the way to the soul level and beyond.

By developing a relationship with ourselves, we learn what is ours to acknowledge and heal, cultivating more energy and higher Love frequencies, and raising the vibration within our physical, mental, emotional, and energetic bodies. Once we have tackled "known" tendencies that are rooted in a lack of Love, we are ready to reveal our unknown aspects. As we heal and rediscover our unique energetic signature as The Love That We Are, we are more stable in our Love, and our practice of being Love.

You may begin working with Tukhmanaha by using the meditation at the beginning of this book. This Light Code assists you in bringing to the forefront of your mind the energies you need to be aware of and review. Once you have entered a meditative state, gaze upon the Light Code. Ask for clarity about the areas within and around your being that need acknowledgment, shifting, balancing, forgiveness, and releasing. Be open to how this information comes to you, as every experience working with Light Codes is different. Unconscious energies can be more elusive, so be patient with yourself and the unveiling process.

Ahakama-ka

(A-ha-ka-ma-ka)

AWAKENING THE HEART

*To have access to your heart is
to have access to your soul.*

The time has come for you to continue your journey into the sacred space of the heart. Regardless of how much or how little "heart work" you have done in the past, you are being guided to continue deepening your travels now. This energetic center is the bridge between the physical and spiritual realms and helps our body anchor fresh energies as directed by our Love. The heart is multilayered, multidimensional, and holds great wisdom as it is directly connected to our soul. It is the center of transformation, and our ultimate guide as we go about our lives. The heart also plays an integral role in generating our energy field. It helps to balance our nervous system, assists us in expanding our intuitive abilities, and plays a key role in all levels of connection with ourself and others.

The heart is powerful, even when tasked with transmuting a tsunami of emotional energies. No matter how much or how often we may experience heartache, our heart can heal, and the connection to our heart is always available to us. Nurturing our connection with our heart grows our connection with our Love and increases our ability to witness the sacred in every situation.

The wisdom of our heart guides us through dark and challenging times, and through these times, the heart seeks greater levels of understanding and acceptance. Love is discerning, and when we are in touch with our heart, we can grow in our skills of discernment. We are moving into a time in which there is more information available to us than there is wisdom, making connecting to this center more important than ever. It is for each of us to connect with our hearts so we can be in tune with the fluctuating, changing energies. As a lightworker, awakening your heart to new levels will serve you in ways you have yet to imagine.

Ahakama-ka can be used with heart opening and healing ceremonies. Perhaps a beautiful cacao ceremony (see below) will resonate for you. Otherwise, the usual meditation techniques or other ways you are guided will suffice.

Cacao Ceremony with Light Codes

Make sure you aren't in a rush, so you can be present with the energies. If possible, use ceremonial-grade cacao. Pure essential oils such as rose, geranium, and sweet orange are recommended, but optional. This ceremony calls for placing oils on the body, so please choose oils that work for you, or omit this direction. You will also need a mug, a simple altar space, a candle, a lighter, and this Light Code.

Directions

Warm up the cacao on the stove at low-medium temperature with some water or milk. If you like, you can add your cacao, hot water, or milk to a blender. Add a couple of drops of rose oil (or your choice of essential oil that is safe for consumption) to the pot or blender. Stir or blend, adding milk or hot water until you reach your preferred consistency. Pour cacao into a special mug. Take your mug, oils, and Light Code to your altar.

Place the mug, oils and Code on your ceremonial altar. While lighting your candle (please refer to safety tips), offer thanks for this opportunity to work with the precious cacao, oils, and Light Code. Now ask for what you would like in relationship to awakening, connecting, and healing your heart. Conclude your prayer as you wish ("So it is," "A-ho," "Amen," etc.).

Place a drop of geranium or sweet orange on your finger, and rub it on your heart space, inhaling the precious aromas. If you have sensitive skin, or would prefer not to place oil on your chest, inhale the fragrance from the dropper bottle, place three drops onto a tissue and inhale, or diffuse it into the air with a mister.

Hold the mug close to your heart. Close your eyes. Breathe in the cacao's and oils' scents. Connect with the energies of the healing cacao plant. Continue holding your intentions as you breathe deeply. Sip the cacao, holding your clear intentions. Maintain a receptive state of mind. As you sip your cacao, gaze at the Light Code. When you are finished, lie down for as long as you need to integrate the energies.

Kalukalei

FEELING THE HEART

*There is a beautiful synergistic relationship
between the physical function of the
heart and the energy and consciousness
which emanates from this sacred center.*

Expanding our connection and understanding of all that the heart center represents assists us in connecting to all parts of ourselves, including the mental, emotional, physical, and spiritual bodies. The heart is far more than a mechanical organ. It is an entire energy center designed to give and receive information, transmute energies, and connect our physical body with Spirit. Yet, consider for a moment the importance and symbolism of the beating, physical heart, the signal of life within the physical vessel. It pumps life-giving blood throughout the body and produces a powerful electromagnetic field. The electromagnetic field conveys information about our emotional state, broadcasting it into space for others to sense and feel, like music playing on a radio. Its rhythm can effect a calm or excited state of being, not only in our own body, but for others within a certain radius of our energy field as well.

There is a beautiful, synergistic relationship between the physical function of the heart and the energy and consciousness which emanates from this sacred center. The heart takes on a big role for human beings, and unfortunately, often it is overshadowed by the less noble construct of the ego.

As we grow up and mature in our modern society, we learn to give the ego authority over the heart. We learn to value the ego's opinion over the heart's innocence and wisdom. It is important that we choose (and continue to choose) to relieve the ego of roles it was not designed to fill. We can now direct the ego to bow further to the greatness of the heart. This Light Code is not only assisting us in calling the heart forward, deepening our connection, and releasing traumas, it is elevating the heart so it can be our best guide, advising the ego rather than the other way around. Since our egos have (to some degree) been in charge, we haven't been able to receive counsel from the wise, sacred aspect of our heart consistently or at the level we might desire. We have misunderstood a lot of events in our lifetimes, as we processed energy through the lower vibrational, fear-based ego-mind. This misunderstanding wounds our hearts, erecting walls of protection. This Light Code will help dissolve these barriers around the heart and help you feel and expand into this space.

There are three meditations for working with this Light Code. Please follow your intuition regarding those that will work best for you.

For Healing and Removing Barriers:

1 Begin by feeling into your feet, practicing the grounding meditation. Slow your breath. When you are ready, gaze upon the symbol. Ask the Code to help release, neutralize, and balance all misqualified energies and lack of love around all levels of your heart.

2 For guiding the ego into its rightful position: Practice grounding. Slow your breath. Gaze upon the symbol and ask the essence of your ego to step forward. Thank the ego for its service. It has worked too hard in a role for which it wasn't designed. Tell the ego it's time to rest and resume its rightful position—as an assistant, working at the heart's direction and guidance. See, sense, and feel the ego bowing to the heart.

3 You may also use this Code with a general meditation. Ask to deepen your connection to your heart.

Tokomataiya

(To-ko-ma-tai-ya)
MIRACLE-MINDED

*It is life-changing to observe
all that is as a miracle.*

This is a time of significant change for Gaia and our solar system, and we human beings are experiencing turbulence that challenges us on many levels. It is imperative that we become more conscious of our thoughts, especially when we work hard to raise our vibration (and carry more energy) and want to manifest consciously our lives. Positive thinking and a positive mindset are key components of a successful life, along with gratitude, security, and what it means for an individual to experience and manifest a joy-filled life.

We human beings are manifesting and creating constantly, but what we manifest, how, and how much are details we can miss easily. The mind can connect with a wide range of frequencies and vibrations. This is one of the many reasons human beings are capable of great things. However, the range of frequencies we harness shows the level of self-mastery we embrace currently. It's easy to forget that the mind plays a key role in controlling our thoughts and emotional processing, all of which affect our manifesting ability. It takes energy to manifest. If we lose energy through upset emotions or dysfunctional thinking, our ability to manifest will be impeded. Or at least we won't manifest or attract what we truly desire.

Having a positive perspective on life will help keep your vibration high. High vibrations make manifesting positive outcomes easier, since manifesting within our 3D, dense, physical realm takes a lot of energy. The human mind is capable, and it can connect with many realms, frequencies, and potentials. We can train the mind to seek favorable conditions, energies, and outcomes, depending on our personal wants, needs, and desires. By using our miracle-minds, we can collapse time, change timelines, and make connections with energies that support our desired outcomes. A miracle is a positive or awesome outcome, especially one that emerges from an impossible or unlikely situation. However, we need not be in dire straits to experience a miracle. For example, the birth of a child is a miracle—it is an extraordinary feat and a manifestation of consciousness and Love. Wouldn't it be life-changing if we could all see *all of life* as a miracle? After all, every person, plant, animal, rock, river, and event is a miracle. Everything we experience is extra-ordinary, but we have become dull and numb—and that prevents us from keeping our vibrations high, and remaining aware of what the energy within and around us is doing. We struggle to remain open, and it can be easy for our senses to become overwhelmed or for the body to feel fatigued.

The amazing thing about the human body is its incredible ability to adapt and heal. In life, there is a lot of data to take in and process. If your upbringing didn't teach you how to assimilate and work with energies, or if you have become contaminated by pollutants (most of us have), it can be difficult for your body to be the sensitive, intelligent antenna it was designed to be. Therefore, you need to focus, ask Spirit, and try to restore and develop your miracle-mindedness. No matter what physical, mental, emotional, or spiritual state you are in, you can develop the habits, thoughts, and behaviors that are beneficial to your fullest expression.

You are capable of great things. This Light Code helps expand your mind and align your body to the infinite potential and experience of miracles. Remember, miracles are around us every moment of every day. Miracles can be big or small, life-enhancing, and life-changing. This mindset, as you open to it, will help you connect with energies that are natural to you.

Please follow the meditation at the beginning of the book to work with this Light Code. It's helpful to imagine the awe and wonder a child or baby animal has when it explores the world. See if you can remember what it was like to be intrigued by the simplest of things . . . such as an ant crawling along the pavement, or the petals of a flower. You may notice your heart swell as you consider these memories, or as you observe something in the room you're sitting in. When you're ready, proceed to your meditation practice, holding the feelings of awe, wonder, inspiration, or bedazzlement you have created inside you. Gaze upon the Light Code and ask for these feelings to become a greater part of your life as you embrace your own miracle mind.

Buhubaha-ha

(Boo-hoo-ba-ha-ha)
COMPASSION FOR ALL

*With growing compassion comes
growing awareness and consciousness.*

For many people, no matter how many times we are told we are not alone, being human can feel lonely and isolating. You inhabit a physical body and are given an ego for experiencing what it is to come to know yourself as an individual part of a whole. However, the individual experience is so convincing that even when we are told we are not alone, we can still feel we are! It's remarkable that we inhabit a planet with seven billion other human beings, and countless insects, birds, critters, and other species, yet we can still feel alone. The remedy for this aspect of the human condition? Compassion for all life.

When we feel compassion for anyone other than ourselves, our heart seeks connection with another heart. We reach out instinctively, our hearts opening to take another being into our energy field. Compassion is a powerful emotion—so powerful it is almost impossible to feel lonely. With enough compassion, you can sit alone in your home with so much company, you may wish for some solitude!

With growing compassion comes the development of self-love. Everything we do is not only for the self, but it encompasses the greater good as well. Compassion leads you to the truth of the collective, interconnected consciousness. Eventually, you know everyone and everything you interact with and relate to is you. Every being is another expression of the divine, and *you* are the divine. Consider for a moment that loneliness is nothing more than a disconnect from yourself. It is a symptom of a lack of self-love, and a disconnect from Love itself.

If you struggle to feel self-love and compassion, this is likely because you are afraid of opening or exposing your heart. Perhaps your heart was wounded, perhaps you struggle even to locate your heart because you have built protective walls around it. If this is the case, please work with the previous Light Codes Ahakama-ka, Awakening the Heart or Kalukalei, Feeling the Heart, until you feel more connected to your heart space. If you are unsure whether you should return to a previous Light Code, remember the Codes will offer you what you need today. There is no one Light Code too advanced or too simple for anyone, as they will continue to offer something useful. Continue with Buhubaha-ha when you are ready.

Choose something close to you with which you would like to connect. It can be another person, a plant, a rock, an animal, a fish, a bug... whatever you like and whatever calls your heart forward. This Code offers you energies to help you bridge where you are now, to a deeper knowing that all things are connected, and all things are One...

thus, relieving loneliness. Once you have chosen with whom (or what) you wish to connect, deepen your breath. Ground yourself. Place your hands over your heart. Imagine expanding the energies of your heart as you breathe in through your heart space, and compressing the energies of your heart space as you exhale. Breathe here for a moment. Call to mind a time when you really wanted to help someone in need, a time when you could sense someone's suffering and you sought to relieve their pain, or a time when you called your compassion forward. As you search your memory, breathe in and out, connecting to your heart space, then gaze upon Buhubaha-ha. The symbol will assist you in cultivating, remembering, and enhancing your compassion. Once you feel ready, call to mind the person, animal, or thing with which you wish to connect, and direct your compassion to them, knowing their heart will receive it instantly. Breathe. Feel more compassion with every breath. Feel the connection strengthening. This connection always has and always will be there. You just need to embrace it. When you feel complete, thank the Light Code, knowing you may practice this meditation at any time.

If you didn't feel a strong connection this time, please go back to Ahakama-ka or Kalukalei, to practice opening and connecting with your heart. If you feel lonely or disconnected from Spirit or Source, meditate on this Light Code or use the exercise above to assist you in remembering the connection.

Tookamen

(Too-ka-men)
HUMANITY IN BALANCE
WITH DARKNESS

Humanity thriving in accordance with
Love is a vision for each of us to hold.

A long, long time ago, humanity transcended much of the darkness that influenced the planet and lived in a heightened vibrational state of coherence. Humanity healed and resolved many wounds, and we had accepted and integrated much of our divine expressions of Love. It is possible to create this utopia again, and it is a vision lightworkers hold today.

As someone seeking to be a conscious creator of their life, you are taking on the role of transcender, doing your part in bringing in the New Age. You are working tirelessly to let go of all that no longer serves you and the collective, consciously and unconsciously, on levels and planes of which you may be unaware. You are a Light bearer, a Light-worker, a noble Knight of the Light, a Seeker of Truth, and a Being of Love. You can bring into your consciousness and awareness the possibility that humanity can live free of pain and suffering. Although low-vibrational darkness never fully leaves us (due to the natural balance between

Light and Dark), we can come to understand its tactics, actions, and deceit. We learn to sense it, to smell it a mile away, so we can choose to align with Love. In fact, we need darkness in order to work with the Light, for without low-vibrational darkness, we cannot know its opposite. However, we need not dwell on the polarities, experiencing extremes all the time. As with all things in nature, there are cycles, and humanity has lingered long enough in the cycle of extremes. Now we hold the space for the frequency of this planet to ascend to a higher plane once again, and to experience a cycle of time in a higher vibration. This plane is aligned with life and the living, and in those higher realms, death and dying serve only in accordance with the natural Law of Love.

You may work with this Light Code to assist yourself in moving into this higher frequency of existence, and you may also offer the energies and consciousness of this Code to the planet and all who inhabit her.

You may use the meditation at the beginning of this book to meditate upon this Code. You may also use it in ceremony, as you feel is appropriate. Perhaps you would like to use this symbol with astrology, and allow your intuition, your heart, and your higher aspects to guide you. Hold the vision of this new world close to your heart, and when you witness a struggle, offer it to others.

This Code is an Ultimate Ascension Code for this planet and it will help you raise your consciousness to the next level, then the level after that, to infinity. You can work with this Code forever (as you can work with all Light Codes).

They will offer you new levels of healing and advancement as you become ready for them.

All blessings on your journey, dear one. We are grateful for your bravery and presence.

Kamatsukra

(Ka-ma-tsu-kr-a)

LIFE PASSION

*Passion is the essence of life and the flow
of energy one experiences while living.*

When someone feels as though they are struggling with any aspect of life (e.g., finances, job success, personal happiness, etc.) that person's relationship with the natural flow of the universe is strained. Often, this tension stems from the activation of new karmic energies (unbalanced energies our soul endeavors to neutralize within our life), or the continued experience of unresolved karmic energies. The purpose of karma is to teach us lessons, and to help us maintain a relative energetic equilibrium within our soul, and with our ancestors, the planet, and the collective consciousness. The lessons we are here to learn vary in difficulty and relate directly to our own individual perception, skill set, and nature. When we feel overwhelmed by life's lessons (e.g., shadow energies, false beliefs, or other energies with which we have "chosen" to interact), the natural Universal flow of energy we require to be happy, healthy, and balanced becomes restricted. We can experience a heavy heart, depression, anxiety, mood disturbances, and other symptoms that reflect a lack of abundance and Love. Having a passion for life can help increase and restore Universal energy flow within our being toward its optimal state. Our interests become clearer, and we can create a general excitement for life! This is not unlike the common relationship expression "the honeymoon phase," wherein Love is flowing and is shared in abundance with someone special.

We can experience the honeymoon phase in any aspect of life, and this is what Kamatsukra represents and offers to you. Are there aspects of yourself you can bring into a positive energy space and flow? Life has a way of testing our resolve and resilience, so it's important to develop a personal toolkit of methods and techniques that can help us through challenging moments. Remember, every obstacle, karmic lesson, shadow, or belief has a positive intent: to help us learn, grow, and expand our consciousness and awareness.

This Light Code is a natural energy generator, showing us through the internal spiral within a circle how to be energy generators ourselves. While we typically understand explosion as a source of energy, with Kamatsukra, *implosion* is the generator of energy.

This Light Code teaches us not only how to be generators of our own energy but also how to connect the many so-called external generators, such as food, water, E energy, and solar energy, all the way up to Source energy. Of course, this is only considered "external" when we are in a separated state of mind.

Kamatsukra can also help us with the release and expansion of energies, by assisting us with letting go of what no longer serves us, and helping us to move into a new, positive space. It holds the frequency and patterns for our life's passions, which, as noted, we can regard as honeymoon energy.

To work with this Code, you may use the usual meditation techniques found at the beginning of this book.

Tumahuma

(Too-ma-hoo-ma)

CONNECTING WITH
SPIRIT GUIDES

*Your spirit guides are
always available to you.*

Often, messages from guides begin with a friendly reminder that we are loved and supported, and that we are not alone. These messages are truths, no matter in what life circumstance you may find yourself. Sometimes, our spirit team can intervene in our life, by setting up circumstances that protect us from danger, or forestalling events that are not aligned with our soul's purpose. Spirit walks with us as a gentle, loving friend, offering wisdoms and nudges that support the life our soul came to experience.

At any given time, there are a few spirit guides working with us. Some guides come, some go, others walk with us for a lifetime. As our interests and passions change, different guides come forward to support those changes. These specialized guides help us learn (or remember) certain skill sets, especially if they are important to our soul's life mission.

Spirit guides exist within a specific frequency range, and we require the help of different guides (temporarily or for an extended period), depending on the realms, levels, and frequencies into which our being connects or expands. As our frequency changes, and we expand our ability to work with a wider range of frequencies, we gain access to these different "levels" of guidance. Some guides will "grow" with us as they work on their own energies and projects.

Feeling, sensing, or communicating with guides brings comfort to many people. Your guides are always available and with you. They love and support you and encourage you to call on them for help. They want to have a relationship with you and want you to understand their sacred connection with you. This Light Code assists you in developing and deepening a connection with your spirit guides.

When calling on your guides, it's important to be specific. If you have a name for one or more of your guides, use their names when you call on them. If you don't have names for your guides (many people don't), say, "Beings of Love and Light who support me." If you feel unsure when communicating with them, you can include, "... in the highest order of Divine Love."

If you want to develop a relationship with your guides as part of your daily self-care practice, set aside a few minutes to work on this relationship. Choosing the same time of day can help, as can working with your birth time because at your birth time, the veil is thin for you between this earthly plane and the spirit realms. For example, if you were born at 2:34 a.m., you could set aside time at 2:34 a.m. or p.m. (the a.m./p.m. is not significant). Your actual birthday is a potent time to connect with guidance too, and to invoke positive energies for manifesting in the year ahead.

You can ask your guides to arrange for energies that are aligned with your optimal life to flow to you.

You can work with this Light Code in a few different ways. You can use the basic meditation at the beginning of this book, or, if you have your own meditations for connecting with your guides, work with those, and include this Light Code to enhance the experience. Otherwise, ground, feel into your heart, gaze upon the symbol, and ask your guide to place their hand on your shoulder. Breathe deeply, relax, and allow your senses to intensify while tuning in to your feeling body.

You can also use this symbol to enhance your channeling of the written or spoken word. First, ground. Tune in to your heart. Gaze upon the Light Code and ask to be open to spoken or written messages from Spirit in accordance with Love. Choose whichever feels natural for you. Relax. Breathe slowly and deeply. Feel the energetic presence of your guide(s). Practice until you can put pen to paper and let words flow, or until you can speak. If you feel stuck, go back to your breath and to the symbol. This skill takes practice and patience . . . but it can be life-changing, so it's worth persevering.

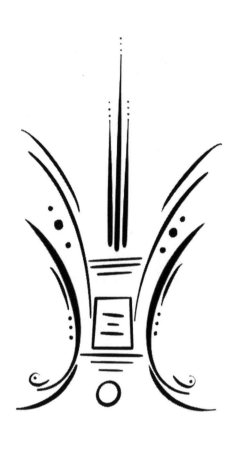

Tieyasako

(Tie-ya-sa-ko)

ALIGN WITH YOUR TRUE SELF,

ALIGN WITH YOUR ENERGY

*Almost all pain and suffering can be
traced back to the pivotal moment
of detaching from one's authentic self.*

So much of the spiritual journey involves healing past traumas and events so we can feel our whole self once again. We often realize how out of touch we are when something unsettling happens, and the illusion we are living in comes crashing down around us. Life is about learning who we are, who we are not, and who we came here to be. However, this simple notion is complex, depending upon how much or how little consciousness we embody.

Almost all pain and suffering can be traced back to the pivotal moment of detaching from one's true self. A long time ago, Source consciousness altered its relationship with all souls to include free will. This new freedom for souls was an offering of Love, but many souls received the gift as abandonment. This misunderstanding is the root cause for many false belief systems, pain, and suffering because, in that moment, many souls forgot who they are (they forgot their authentic self). For more information on this pivotal moment in our creation history, please refer to our book *Light Codes for the Soul*. The authentic self is aligned with the universe, full of energy and in harmony with Love. It *is* Love. But we might wonder, if a being resonates with Love, how could they experience trauma? How could they not be aligned to their calling and destiny? How can they not have everything they need? The universe supports those who walk in *their* Love, full of *their* energy, where the words "trauma and upset," or "frustration and anger" can't make as strong a disturbance for them. It doesn't mean one can't feel these emotions—they are part of the human experience—but these emotions can move through the body unrestricted, and can be processed in a healthy, Loving way.

Emotions such as frustration and upset create a specific vibratory pattern in the body, and occur when we forget the Truth of who we are. If we continue practicing these emotions in excess, eventually we establish an attractor field for similar and habitual responses. For example, when we lose something we care about (such as a job or a partner), we feel traumatized, and may feel rejection, abandonment, or some other lack of Love. How traumatized we feel depends on how much we seek outside ourselves to fill the void of Love we believe we are missing. Somewhere along the way, we (hopefully) learn that we need not take anything personally. So, little "hurt" or "rejection" can ensue because we never abandoned the Truth of who we are. We never abandoned our Love. It doesn't mean life is easy, but those who are called to align with their consciousness and their true self will find that challenging emotions and energies are easier to process when we approach them in an appropriate, masterful manner.

When we experience an upsetting event, it is helpful to remember that there is a positive intent in every situation.

Some examples of why a job or person leaves our life are:

- to bring us back into alignment with self.
- a karmic relationship ending, or
- a necessary soul experience ending.

When we are still in the phase of understanding that we are here to experience and learn, we perceive such events as "tests." When we transcend this level of consciousness, and move into a higher level of experience, we discover that there are no tests . . . there are only experiences of Love leading us back to our self.

Eventually, as we heal and increase our vibration, we discover there is a level of consciousness that honors and accepts all energies, including energies we might consider as dark or evil. Please allow us to explain. The Universe (God, Source, Creator) has an unlimited number, variety, and range of frequencies, from low to high to infinity in all directions. The Creator gives a soul free will when it incarnates on this planet, as determined by Universal Law. To know itself more deeply, a soul may need to behave in a manner that causes disruption to others. A soul may have karmic or other contracts that cause it to engage with others in ways that affect them positively or negatively. Because of a conflict between their needs and the needs of an influential soul, people may judge a situation, take things personally, or fall out of alignment with their Love. When we take things personally (forgetting who we are), we perpetuate a cycle of pain and suffering. However, if a soul needs to express themselves (whether it be for karmic reasons or for a simple experience), and the recipient of their actions reacts with compassion and forgiveness, healing can occur. If the recipient of an event understands that "this person's soul is exercising its free will, playing out something that is important for them," that reaction lessens (or potentially heals) the cycle of pain and suffering for all parties involved with the event. There is no further disruption.

⸎

The Light Code Tieyasako is holding the space and energy for you to choose to respond differently to difficult situations and to connect with the truth of who you are, so you can become stronger in this truth and walk on this planet with compassion, forgiveness, and grace. This Code also assists with aligning your energy, so the challenges you face will have less of a difficult impact as you become stronger in knowing who you are. The meditation at the beginning of this book partners well with this Light Code. Meditate upon this Light Code, either with a specific challenge in mind to help move energy into its appropriate place, or use this Code to expand your connection with self.

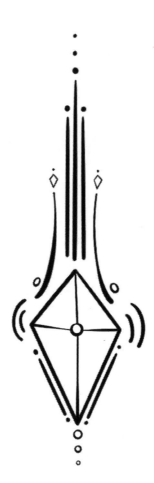

Piyahama

(Pie-ya-ha-ma)
STANDING FIRM IN MY LOVE

Love, by nature, is a
powerful, unwavering force.

Love is powerful and defined, yet is soft and flexible. Love knows how to respond to every situation, never losing integrity or authority. Its sympathetic nature provides nurturing and healing, and supports all of life. On the highest level, every being is created in Love; with and by the energy of Love. Everything in existence is governed, directed, and commanded by Love, and put into action by adamantine particles.

As we discover and learn more about ourselves, we realize we aren't standing in our inner authority and power consistently. To stand in our power means we have connected with and integrated The Love That We Are. When we know our Love, we become an immovable force that our Love commands, yet we are responsive, centered, forgiving, and, of course, loving. We know within our being that we are powerful, and that knowing is rarely, if ever, shaken. Integrating these truths is the essence of knowing oneself, and some may say it is our greatest test or challenge in living a human life. If one were to integrate their Love, they would master their being and be a master of this dense, 3D realm.

Rather than giving our power away, let us focus on knowing ourselves, standing in our Love, and becoming the Masters that we are. This takes self-reflection, healing, unlearning, deprogramming, opening to give and receive energy without restriction, and letting go of resistance, fear, and shame (and all the other false beliefs we have gained over lifetimes). It's quite a task—or some may believe it is. However, the potential exists for each of us to leave it all behind and step into the divine, sublime, true nature of our Love.

All the baggage we carry is a choice we made somewhere along the way. We can get caught up with "he said this," or "she did that," and believe we are victims of horrible, unloving acts (which happen, especially when we are disconnected from Love). However, it is our choice to carry feelings and memories of upset or discordant energy. Remember, all of our anguish has happened in the past, and anything we believe is forthcoming is simply a projection of our minds. The question becomes: when will we drop our upset, confusion, victimhood, fear, etc., and take an active step into our own Divine Light? This task is challenging, for as we know, we human beings hold false beliefs and programs about who and what we are. We can all feel confused about how to heal and let go of an upsetting event or issue, let alone know how to include the healing on multiple levels, timelines, dimensions, or realities. When we haven't healed an issue on all levels, that issue's energy repeats as a lesson until, eventually, we release that energy pattern. We may, for example, engage in the same type of dysfunctional relationships until we heal the energy that supports such attractions. However, even if we can't connect to all levels when we heal, we continue to raise our vibration, attracting positive situations and relationships that assist our healing process. We learn to rise out of "mucky" lower vibrational patterns and gain perspective. This practice creates space for our authentic nature—our *Love,* to be more fully embodied into our conscious being. As we heal, we don't go as deep into or stay as long in upset or confusion because Love aligns and directs us. Our base frequency is higher because we are aligned with our Love.

This Code holds the energetic signature for you to anchor yourself in your Love. The more you integrate your Love, the broader, richer, and clearer perspective you will have about life and your future. The more you are open to your Love, the easier it will be to negotiate situations, to assist others, and to be yourself. Opening to Love is cyclical. The more we heal, the easier it is to connect to our Love. The more Love we have, the easier it is to heal and command our adamantine particles.

Meditate upon this Code, using the meditation at the beginning of this book. Invite awareness and consciousness in, and integrate more of the Love That You Are.

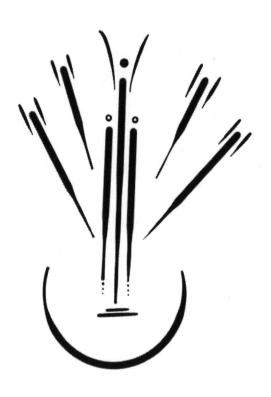

Hoyakama

(Ho-ya-ka-ma)

BE WHO YOU CAME HERE TO BE

You are the entire universe.

Perhaps you are aware you have a wonderful life mission and purpose. To embrace our mission and purpose, it is important that we discover and integrate our authentic nature on as many levels as possible. You didn't come here simply to be someone's child, work a job, and pay taxes. You came here to find truth, and this book is here to help you find it—not only your truth, but the truth of the universe. Let's become aware of and release the programming that shackles our minds, and free the great potential each of us holds. We can realize, on a cellular level, right down to the adamantine particles and baseline energy of our existence, what we are and who we came here to be. These realizations and healings of the mind and the body are instrumental to grounding the truth of our being (our Love) into our current 3D experience.

Our living experience is made possible by our incredible physical body, which holds all the information in the universe. You are a walking memory stick. This information is stored in your tissues... right in your DNA. The body, as a divine expression of the soul, is connected to all things in existence, including past, present, and future energies. The body has the potential to harness an unlimited array of energies as we learn how to connect to the Infinite. Therefore, it is helpful to include statements to acknowledge healing on as many levels as possible, such as "... across all timelines, all dimensions, all realities, for all ancestors, and in the DNA."

It's also important that we take the time to observe the many falsities we've learned over the course of our current (and potentially past) lifetimes. We do this by noticing (without judgment) our reactions and even question societal norms. Not everything we have learned is useful for our journey toward self-mastery. The mind has many limitations, so it is important to acknowledge that the mind won't be able to comprehend everything. As the mind typically learns linearly, it can be challenging for us to override old knowledge with new knowledge. As we walk our spiritual path, we encounter many notions which at first glance seem too unlikely, illogical, improbable, or even possible. It can feel as though our minds are a steel rod we are attempting to bend with bare hands! As we move forward with the understanding that there are times when the mind will feel strained to understand a concept contrary to what it learned in the past, we can hold patience in our hearts for the mind's advancement. Our heart knows the truth and it can offer support and encourage our minds to trust and remain open to the reality beyond our 3D knowledge and experience.

Some people find it challenging to work past false limitations, to expand their minds, and to contact their true self. The time is ripe to make a consciousness shift on this planet, so everyone can connect to their sacred truth and feel Spirit's support in doing so. Imagine a world in which everyone is living in alignment with the truth of who they are, flourishing in abundance and happiness, and at one with the natural world.

Today, we begin with you, dear soul. We are honored and grateful that you are interested in and dedicated to not only improving your life, but—as an incredible byproduct of healing—the lives of everyone incarnated now and in other timelines. When you realize who and what you are, everything makes perfect sense. You see a greater picture. You have compassion. Forgiveness abounds, and life is a very different experience. As you continue down the path of self-realization, Spirit may show you your genuine connection to yourself and Source. It is helpful, therefore, to take small steps—like working with this Light Code—to prepare your mind for this quantum leap in consciousness.

This Light Code assists and empowers your connection to yourself. Be gentle with this process. It has the potential to be life-changing! Remember, you must learn to crawl before you can walk, and walk before you can run. Forcing connections will not work, as they can strain your being, restricting your connection to your Love. If you notice any feelings, such as pressure, frustration, or longing, take a break. Recenter. Do a meditation of your choice or use the Six Direction Meditation at the beginning of this book.

Come back to this Light Code often as you progress through this book. Meditate with this Code and with its affirmation (see below) anytime you feel ready to connect with yourself. If you are struggling in life (such as with a loss, an illness), if you are anxious or depressed, or if you are otherwise in search of a stronger connection to Self,

Spirit, and Source, meditate upon this Code.

Take your time. You may make connections with Truth, and lose them. There is nothing wrong with you. Our modern lifestyle rarely supports this connection. Come back to this Code when you need to be reminded of that.

꩜

When ready, gaze upon the Light Code. After you've connected with the energy of the Code, use the affirmation below (or use your own). Feel the words and the energy you speak, along with the energy of the Code.

Light Code Affirmation:

"I choose to be who I came here to be."

Utahmaka

(Ooo-tah-ma-ka)
GROWING IN CONSCIOUSNESS
AND AWARENESS

*Growing in consciousness and awareness
is achieved by increasing one's ability
to expand, contract, and focus one's energy.*

You may notice there are phases of self-discovery in your relationship to self and others. Throughout this time of development, people can swing like a pendulum into extremes: becoming self-focused and even narcissistic, not considering people or things outside of themselves. At the opposite end of the spectrum, they can avoid self by focusing on others. On a spiritual path, you can experience both extremes.

Once someone acknowledges wounds, traumas, false beliefs, etc. within themselves that need healing, and begins the healing process, often there is a time of self-absorption. It is sometimes a necessary process, both for those who find it easy to focus on themselves and for those who avoid self-focus. However, both extremes can be positive and necessary for a period, as deep healing can occur on the personal level and for all of humanity.

At some point, seekers realize that the healing they do for themselves can affect others positively as well—one's close circle of family and friends, acquaintances, and the collective at large. A slow expansion and refocusing of one's consciousness begins. One focuses on one's own energy, healing, autonomy, and on building a greater connection and understanding of all parts of the self.

When done well, self-focus builds coherent energy, an energy that is soft and strong, balanced and unified. Then, the seeker can use their energy to expand and make more connections or "contact points" outside of their usual conscious, energetic, and spiritual reach. The expansion and focusing of energy is how we "grow in our consciousness and awareness."

We need connection with other people at both ends of the spectrum: when we are feeling self-focused, and when we are feeling expansive, as our energy bodies and consciousness reach further across the universe. If one is exploring their own energy and inner world, interaction with others is still important. An impartial person's perspective (or energy) could be a catalyst for magic in your journey toward increased consciousness. The same goes for someone in an expansive period. We need contact with others, especially new people, during an expansive time so we can reach far into the quantum field of collective consciousness to connect and learn! We can also share with other people, verbally and energetically, what we know, and that sharing can assist us in our own and others' personal development.

The contact points come from expanding our mind in new ways, to include concepts, information, and potential to which we haven't had access previously. We might feel contact points as a sensation in our brain, like a spark of light, or a light bulb turning on, or we might feel excited when we converse with someone on a level that speaks to us. Conversations and interactions that stretch your limits, blow your mind, and energize you are food for your soul.

We can feel excited and overly ambitious as we seek new ways to grow on all levels of our being. We can feel tired and in need of more rest, quiet time, and seclusion. Growing in our consciousness and awareness is like an acrobatic exercise for the body, mind, and soul. It can be an exhausting process to heal, expand our minds, and integrate the fresh energies we discover. Therefore, it is important to take a break from intense growth from time to time. These breaks differ from being stuck or stagnant. Breaks can create room for us to breathe and allow us to pursue an interest or passion, which may be an important detour on the soul's journey. Life may also need our attention for a time, as "life" happens. Our being may also need time to rest, integrate, or rejuvenate before moving on to the next task or "level" of awakening. Even if we feel like we need to retract from life, like a turtle pulling into its shell, it's still preferable to remain open to universal direction and flow, as there are always more opportunities and connections to discover.

Once we experience this cycle of expansion and contraction a few times, we might understand how deeply we are all connected, that we are "One." On all levels (including in the 3D realm), we *are* One. There is just one fish. There is just one dog. There is just one human. Then we take it further... to there is just One. Your experience is part of the One's experience. Your thoughts and feelings are part of the One's thoughts and feelings. Your pain and suffering is shared by the One. You heal yourself. You heal the One. You show compassion, forgiveness, and gratitude toward yourself; you show it for the One. Your expanding consciousness and awareness are the One's expansion as well.

Contemplate this message to assist the growth of your consciousness and awareness. To work with this Light Code, use the simple meditation at the beginning of the book. Meditate for as long as is appropriate for you.

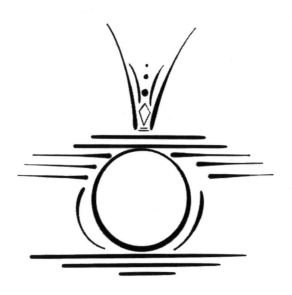

Kamakahai

(Ka-ma-ka-hai)
HIGHER SELF CONNECTION

*Gratitude is a blessed energy that
helps the heart continue to expand.* •

We invite you to tune in to your sacred heart so you
may receive the sweet, powerful connection to your
higher self, that aspect of self that is free of the ego,
and lives in a higher plane. It has a broader perspective,
offering wisdom and guidance in alignment with your soul.
The higher self acts as a bridge between your lower, incarnated aspects and your soul. As we deepen our connection
with the higher self, we align with the soul's mission and
our life's purpose, and improve the flow of Universal energies within our being.

Connecting with the higher self is a powerful step along the path of awakening, and this
connection can always be developed further. The higher
self is sacred, and its perspective is valuable for those
choosing to live aligned with their soul and their Love.
Working with the higher self requires that the ego step
back and kneel to the power of the heart. We contact
our higher self through the heart and crown chakras.

If you don't already converse with your higher self, with practice and an expanding heart, you will likely be able to do so. Remain humble. Remember, this part of you knows far more than your human self can comprehend. Honor this part of you. Hold a feeling of gratitude. Gratitude is a blessed energy that helps the heart expand, allowing you to have a richer connection with this sacred aspect of yourself. You will ask your higher self many things, but it only knows (or shares) what the soul wants you to know. Be open, however, to all your higher self presents to you, using all of your senses.

Begin with the preparatory grounding meditation at the beginning of this book. When you feel grounded and relaxed, gaze upon this Light Code. Feel into your heart space, keeping your breaths full and deep. When you feel ready, affirm in your own words that you choose to connect with your higher self. Ask for Kamakahai's help and the help of the Beings of Light who Love and support you.

Close your eyes. Breathe slowly and deeply. Tune in to your heart space. Feel for a change in your energy. When you notice a shift, ask, "Are you my higher self?" Wait for an answer. If you don't receive one, or didn't grasp the meaning of the answer you received, ask that the answer be offered in a manner you can understand. When you feel confident you have reached your higher self, ask a couple of genuine, heart-felt questions. When you feel complete, thank your guides, your higher self, and the Light Code for their help.

If you weren't able to make contact the first time, try

again. It is common to feel apprehensive or excited. Perhaps your desire for an answer is so strong that it blocks your ability to receive the energy from your higher self or your guides. Be gentle with yourself and with the process, allowing the connections to develop in divine timing. As with any relationship you want to nurture, do not be forceful or demanding. Stand firm in your Love and let go of all predeterminations and expectations. Allow Spirit to direct an orchestra of beautiful and harmonious energies. Be patient. You'll get there.

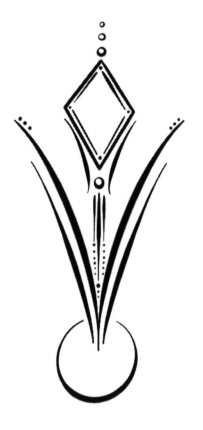

Tulahruma

(Too-lah-ru-ma)
SOUL TO HIGHER
SELF CONNECTION

Step by step, we release what was
never ours, to reclaim what always is.

an we remain aware in a world filled with so many distractions and deceptions?

In this world, we continue to create, just as our ancestors did, manifesting many things, even things we may not intend to manifest. It is up to each of us as an individual to engage with our own energy so we know what our energy is doing, and where our energy is going.

Now, more than ever, seekers like you are called to answer a challenge: to continue to choose to be present and clear, in mind and heart, during this Great Shift—the current changing of the Ages, and the collective shift in Light consciousness. Aware seekers know they have accepted the Shift on a soul level. Our soul wants to expand its vibration, raise the consciousness of our lower egoic self, and embrace its higher aspects. This embrace requires practice, healing, and fine tuning of the programs we allow our ego-minds to run. Remember, each individual is only beset by the challenges they can handle, and each of us develops in our own time frame and in our own way. It's the nature of being human.

Human beings operate on programs which grow into habits and often limit or belittle our eternal connection and power. These habitual patterns dictate how we function in life. Therefore, we must think seriously, both about the programs with which we engage, and about those we release when they are no longer of service to our life or soul mission. When we run programs aligned to our higher aspects, they assist us in behaving like those higher aspects, and we walk the Earth with more understanding, ease, and purpose. When we are mindful and engaged in all aspects of life, our energy increases, and we define our talents and skills. These are all signs that our lower self is expanding and integrating our higher self.

You may choose to connect to your higher self and soul consciously. You can reach energetically higher than your 3D, egoic-mind knows. This "leveling up" can take time, and it is essential to heal the energies that limit your heart's connection and expansion. All of this requires support from your guides, your archangels, and the Ascended Masters.

Meditate upon Tulahruma by starting with the grounding meditation at the beginning of this book. Imagine, feel, and sense breathing with your heart space. Each breath expands your heart space, while each exhale compresses and focuses the expansion perfectly. This exercise is a useful tool for connecting with your higher self. When this becomes easy for you, you may deepen this meditation by closing your eyes and imagining you are a cloud. With all your senses engaged, feel into your cloud-ness. Notice how light you are—a formless, expansive, weightless cloud, contacting the consciousness stream that connects your higher self and soul. Ask the Code and your guides or your favorite Ascended Master to assist you. Be in this beautiful space for as long as you wish. When you feel complete, bring your attention back to your body and the space in which you are sitting.

Because this exercise can unground you, after doing this exercise, it's beneficial to perform the grounding meditation provided at the beginning of this book.

Tulahruma can help you release programs that inhibit your connection to your higher self and soul. One way we can release limiting belief programs is by identifying them, and then replacing the "false program" with a "positive program." If you are aware of your limiting beliefs, you may work on them while asking the Code to assist you in releasing them using your preferred method. Another way of working with limited beliefs is to call to mind a known false belief (e.g., "I am unworthy"). Sit with this statement. What does this mean to you? Without dwelling on it for too long, notice your thoughts and feelings. Gaze upon the Light Code. Ask the Code to help you release the limited belief. Imagine, feel, and sense the release of the belief, like dropping a leaf into a stream and watching the current take it away. Sit with the energy until you feel a release or a lightness come over you. Use your intuition, muscle testing or other technique to confirm that the limited belief is gone. Then affirm a positive statement that is the opposite of the false belief you just released. For example, as you gaze upon the Code, say, "I am worthy." Breathing deeply, repeat the positive statement: "I am worthy" (or whatever positive statement feels appropriate for you). Feel, sense, and imagine the truth in this affirmation for as long as you need. When you feel complete, thank the Light Code, your guides, and the Ascended Masters for their help.

As noted earlier, to banish your limiting beliefs, engage in shadow work. While that complex process is beyond the focus of this book, there are many trustworthy practitioners you can find online. The Codes found in this book will support any shadow/belief work process, and will help you integrate positive, truthful thoughts and beliefs (programs for the ego-mind).

We encourage you, dear one, to take a moment for yourself twice a day for at least three weeks, to tune in to your heart space. Find a quiet space where you can be alone for a minute or two. Imagine and feel as though you are breathing with your heart space. This meditation helps to facilitate a connection with our physical body, as well as our higher aspects.

Tiyakama

(Ti-ya-ka-ma)

HEART AND SOUL-MIND
CONNECTION

*The more we can connect with the heart and
soul-mind, and balance them within our being, the
greater direction and guidance we will receive.*

Establishing a balanced connection between our heart and soul-mind is an important phase in our spiritual development. As the energetic center between the physical and spiritual realms, the heart plays a crucial role in integrating the consciousness of the higher mind (heart and soul-mind) with the physical body. Regardless of the emotional traumas and narratives the heart has accumulated, at its core, the heart is whole and beautiful. However, when we experience trauma, or carry forward a false belief, and the entire chakra system can't process the event or energy, the associated shadow energies can penetrate the heart. Even with the presence of traumatic energies, the heart can maintain its function and keep its connection with the higher mind. The more we heal these traumas, the more we can tune in to the heart and its connection with the soul-mind. Thus, it is of paramount importance that we work to release our shadows and the false beliefs and traumas we have experienced over lifetimes, so we can embrace the power of the heart-soul-mind connection.

While we work with this Light Code, although our being requires more heart healing, we can work on strengthening the sacred connection between the heart and soul-mind. The more we connect with these aspects and balance them in our being, the more neutral and clear direction and guidance we will receive. Our intuition and intuitive accuracy will increase. Our natural gifts and talents will work together to support a soul-fulfilling life.

You may use this Code if you feel confused about life decisions, or if you need clarity—especially from a higher level of consciousness. Tiyakama assists you in developing harmony, coherence, and connection with your higher mind while bringing the wisdom of the higher mind into the physical body where you can use the information and messages.

~☙

This Light Code also offers a special meditation to help those who wish to live a more spiritually connected life and develop an understanding of their heart's great wisdom. Gaze upon the Code and focus on your heart space. While working with the symbol, you may also feel a crown chakra connection (but it's okay if you don't!). Breathe into your heart space. Imagine there are two equilateral triangles hovering parallel to your body. The base of the bottom triangle is located approximately three feet below your feet in the ground, with its top point in front of your heart center. The top triangle is inverted, facing down, with the base of the triangle hovering three feet above your head in space, and the top point meeting the other triangle in front of the heart center. The bottom triangle anchors and grounds the heart connection into the earth, while the top triangle expands the energy upward into the soul (and potentially beyond if you choose consciously to take it there). Using the structure of the triangles, visualize energy from your heart space moving up through the center of your body and out your crown chakra, while the energy from your soul-mind reaches down through your body toward your feet, and into the ground, grounding you. These energies are balanced and integrated in your heart space, where you focus your breath. When you feel complete, release the exercise and offer gratitude for the practice.

Komasoy-yo

(Ko-ma-soy-yo)
SACRED HEART

*To have access to your heart is
to have access to your soul.*

The heart center is multidimensional, comprising levels and layers including the physical heart organ, the energy center of the heart chakra, the lower heart, the sacred heart, and the higher heart. With growing awareness and consciousness, the heart center expands, leading to greater degrees of awareness, understanding, compassion, forgiveness, and exchanges of Love.

The sacred heart lives within the heart chakra, centered in the body behind the physical heart, a couple of inches forward of the spine. A holy energy point, it has access to the soul. It is a place of solace and refuge, a safe space within every being on this planet. It offers everything one requires for living in wisdom, connection, and peace, and for navigating the world. The sacred heart acts as a home and a guide, and allows for healing and connection to the higher aspects of self and the higher realms. The sacred heart is a portal and focus point of the soul within our being.

One can connect with the sacred heart through meditation, and with the help of this Light Code, Komasoy-yo. To work with this Light Code, begin with the grounding practice at the beginning of this book. Once you feel the earth energy flowing through your body, gaze upon Komasoy-yo. Continue to pull the earth's energy up through the bottoms of your feet and bring your attention to your heart space. Rest your hands over your heart space to help focus the energy. Now imagine and feel as though you are breathing with your heart space, expanding and compressing this center with every breath, and moving into the Light Code. As you deepen your connection, and the Code draws you in, you may find your heart opening. In your mind's eye, see yourself in a meadow. In the meadow is a beautiful house. Notice the details of this house. What is it made of? Is it big or small? What are the windows like? Allow the image of this house to form with as much detail as possible, without dwelling on it for too long. There is a path through the meadow that leads to the front door. Of what is the path made? Do any details reveal themselves—are there flowers, bushes, or garden ornaments? Walk up to the house. Open the door—it is the door of your sacred heart. Walk into the house. The space is precious and unique. This is your sacred heart space. Take your time. Explore . . . what do you discover? You may be surprised! When you feel complete, bring your attention back to your breath and to the room you are in. Thank the Light Code for its help.

Working with this Light Code and meditation can help you develop a deeper connection with your heart on multiple levels. There is much to discover, and there are many things you can do within this space. Some people offer themselves or others healing energy, some do soul work, others meet with their guides or simply enjoy the energy. Trust that whatever is revealed to you is what your higher aspects feel is appropriate. This is a sacred space, so enter it with the purest of intentions. Remember, this is your personal, sacred access point—your heart in its finest form. Be gentle. Be humble. Be innocent. From this space, you will receive the great divine energies and all their blessings.

Lolat'kama

(Lo-laa' t'ka-ma)
ADAMANTINE PARTICLES

*This holy particle is full of potential,
vibrating at a high octave, ready to
morph into anything Love would direct.*

In metaphysical circles, adamantine particles are thought to be the smallest particles in existence. Adamantine particles are made of Love and are directed by Love... they *are* Love. They are the foundation of energy, directed and commanded by Love and by Source. The adamantine particle is the reason we can say that Love built our world and everything in it.

These particles are so small and move so quickly they cannot be seen, even with the strongest microscope. They are energy itself and respond to conscious direction in accordance with Love. If we consider our entire being for a moment, the adamantine particle is our foundation: from our highest state of consciousness, to the RNA and DNA that determines what cells grow into various body parts. The adamantine particle is at the foundation of everything with which we interact—from the ground we walk on to the lake or ocean we swim in to the grass, trees, birds, and bees, all the way to the planets and galaxies and beyond. Our homes are built by adamantine particles, as are the clothes we wear, the food we eat... and our thoughts and emotions, too! Everything is energy, and energy is adamantine particles.

When we are in tune with Love and with our world, and are experiencing life from a happy or positive mindset, things go more smoothly for us. Have you ever noticed, when we love our work, how easy it becomes? When we love someone deeply, how much comfort, sweetness, and enjoyment we can share? This is because of the high exchange rate of adamantine particles between one thing and another. It is the refreshing of Love that offers new life or energy to any situation. These tiny particles, as directed by Love (because they *are* Love), bring about healing and resolutions. They are the interconnection between divine rhythms–the space and matter which weaves the entire universe.

Your ability to tap into the ever-flowing river of adamantine particles means you are in harmony with the energy of the world around you. Adamantine particles give structure to this dimension—in fact, they create dimensions and the space between dimensions! Our consciousness can connect with these particles at any moment of any day. In fact, whether or not we are aware of them, we are working with them.

Try this little exercise. Look around you. Notice the space you're in, this book you're reading, the clothes you're wearing, and the body you have. Your command of adamantine particles (mostly on a soul level) has built all of this. Now consider your health, your energy level, and your general happiness. These are indicators of how consciously you are connected to the life-giving stream of adamantine particles. They show how connected you are with your Love. Remember, the adamantine particle is akin to a Love particle.

Now, imagine you could be at complete peace. What

would that look like? What would that feel like? Take a moment and tune in to this thought experiment. Now consider... In what areas of your life are you out of sync with your peaceful vision? These are the same areas you are out of sync with Love and the adamantine particles. This doesn't mean you need to become a monk and retreat up a mountain (although this will be the case for some people), but it offers clues about how you can change your lifestyle to be in alignment with your true nature, and what your true nature desires. After all, your true nature is in harmony with the adamantine particles that Love directs.

Lolat'kama offers you a visual touch point to adamantine particles.

Sit quietly and comfortably, with a pen and paper nearby. Slow your breath. Close your eyes. When you're ready, tune in to your heart space. Contemplate how you are out of sync with your inner peace or Love. Notice how it feels. What images come to mind? What sensations do you feel? Write them down as they come to you. When you are ready to move on, open your eyes. Gaze upon the Light Code. Ask the Code and the Beings of Love and Light who support you to assist you in understanding your interaction with the adamantine particles. What areas in your life need shifting so you can align with these particles?

Ask for these shifts to be set in motion as directed by your highest potential, and as governed by your Love. Be with the energy of your requests and the energy of the Light Code for as long as you require. When you feel complete, thank the symbol, yourself, and the Beings of Love and Light who support you.

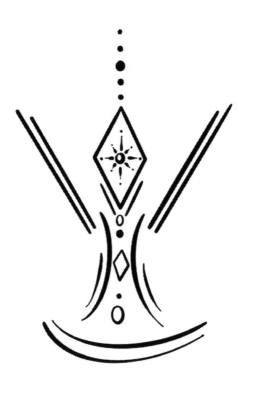

Hosai-eti

(Ho-say-i-ti)

KNOWING YOUR TRUTH

*It's time to transition out of our past and
into the eternal; venturing into the Eternal
Self, as well as into the infinite potential
of both nothingness and superfluity.*

The time has come to deepen our connection to the divine, authentic self once more. This connection is an ongoing process of healing, discovery, and acknowledgment, which can be easy if we are willing and able to see who and what we are.

The statement "human beings have created a lot of false beliefs" is one we reflect upon often in this book because it is significant in the journey back to self. It's important not to place blame on anyone or anything for humanity's dysfunctional programs, for placing blame only perpetuates the cycle of pain and suffering. However, we do not need to linger in past programming. You can now choose, if you haven't already, to spend *more time* developing a connection with your truthful, authentic self, and *less time* healing the past.

Coming to know and embody truth can be a lifelong

exploration. We all have moments of tasting our true nature throughout our lives. The closer we live in this authentic alignment, the more our energy bodies and consciousness can expand, leading us on an adventure to discover some of the complexity of the universe. This discovery of ourselves and the universe includes opening our hearts and minds to the many paradoxes found in the physical, metaphysical, and spiritual worlds.

To know yourself is to live from the heart, to be one with your heart and soul-mind connection, and to be anchored to your higher aspects and your physical experience. (If you need a reminder about the heart and soul-mind connection, please revisit Tiyakama.) Most of us will need to practice expanding, contracting, and compressing the energy from our heart space, which is why we revisit this topic again and again, from different angles. Eventually, we seek to broaden the mind along with the expansion and contraction of the heart, while connecting with the soul, and becoming the sacred witness to the complexities of the universe. We might notice at some point that there truly is "just energy" while simultaneously experiencing the infinite potential of that energy. Energy is infinite potential, yet it can also be nothing at all. This statement can be applied broadly, for our consciousness, inclusive of our heart and soul-mind connection, gives birth to every engagement and experience within ourselves and others throughout our life. Our conscious connection to our heart and soul-mind helps us to remain in a state of self-awareness, highlighting what is true and supportive to our being, and what is not. Unmistakably, we realize our Love is our foundation.

Being in tune with ourselves offers us greater clarity in life, and helps us stay in flow and harmony with all that life presents. We invite you to consider the relationship between truth and clarity. Clarity is the receptivity of the profound knowing and wisdom our higher aspects offer us. Our truth (or our true nature) is a direct reflection of our higher aspects. The relationship between truth and clarity is circular. As one finds clarity, one's truth becomes stronger... and as one's truth strengthens, clarity is revealed. Our embodiment of our higher aspects is reinforced by the embodiment of our truth. Therefore, clarity comes from knowing our truth; from integrating enough of ourselves (our true nature) that we can understand the greater truth of the universe... or the "bigger picture." We still have a life to experience, but we can experience it knowing who and what we are.

Unfortunately, even though we strengthen our inner knowing and truth, not everything in life will be smooth sailing. Life on this planet is messy and filled with confusing, dynamic energies. Navigating life from your truth will give you clarity so you know how to act or not act. You will have stronger clues about the energies you need to address, release, bring into balance, and so on, and because you have clarity, you can accomplish this with fewer disruptions and upset.

Knowing our truth begins by reflecting on our past (past lives, karmic relationships, ancestral energies, false beliefs, thoughts, and notions) and releasing anything that is not of our Love. We take responsibility that we agreed to interact with these energies. Next, we understand that these energies, experiences, and interactions do not define us, nor do they hold power other than the power we give them. We regain our divine power and authority, and move forward into our true being.

With the Light Code Hosai-eti, you can choose, if you wish, to broaden your connection to your authentic, Eternal Self, and integrate new levels of your truth. This act leaves the ego far behind as you enter the realms of the Eternal Self. You realize nothing is as important as it seems, and that you give meaning to everything in this world. It is up to you to decide if you are ready, willing, and able to take command and responsibility for your energy and being.

To work with this Code, create, in your own words, intentions or affirmations that apply to the false beliefs that have been holding you prisoner, and have kept you from understanding who and what you are. Here are a few suggestions . . .

- "I choose to see clearly, with no confusion."

- "I choose to connect more fully with my authentic self."

- "I choose to release all false, preconceived thoughts and beliefs of my reality."

- "I choose to release the program of taking things personally."

- "I choose to become more aware of my programs so I can decide which ones to keep and which to release."

- "I choose to expand my awareness of my false and limiting beliefs, so I can release them by the direction of my Love."

- "I choose to embrace the truth of the universe, in all its infinite potential, for which I am a part."

You may also ask the Code and your guides or higher aspects to help you receive an appropriate affirmation, and then wait to receive this phrase.

When you are ready to work with the symbol, bring your affirmation(s)/intention(s) to the forefront of your mind. Ground and relax using the meditation at the beginning of this book. Feel into your heart, while breathing earth energy throughout your body. Gaze upon the Code to connect with its energies. When you are ready, say your intention(s) while meditating upon the symbol. Feel the energies of the Light Code and your affirmation(s) growing within and around your being. After a few moments, release both the energy of the Code and your intention(s) to the universe, where your higher aspects and Source can address the energies. Thank the Light Code for its help. Relax. Remain aware of your thoughts as you go about your day, and work with this symbol as often as needed.

Potakama

THE ETERNAL SELF

The Eternal Self is a sacred part
of you, protected by its own
generator of Love and innocence.

Take a moment to contemplate the question: "What does 'the Eternal Self' mean to you?" We do not want to impose limitations on your concept of the Eternal Self by offering a definitive and descriptive definition. Instead, we prefer to inspire you to reflect on your own notion of this energy, and then use the suggestions in this section to expand upon what this aspect of self is for you.

The Eternal Self is the infinite parts of you. These energies are entwined with your soul and are, in fact, the greatest aspects of your soul. However, there are also energies in your soul that are *not* eternal—they are transitory experiences and lessons your soul "tries on" to gain wisdom, knowledge, and experience. Some of these energies are integrated into the Eternal Self, becoming One with your infinite aspect, while other, temporary energies are processed and released in Love. The Eternal Self is the aspect of your soul that remains intact for eternity.

You may choose to contact the Eternal Self to gain clarity or enhance your gifts and talents. You can also connect with this aspect to integrate greater levels of understanding of your lower self, regarding your life, life experiences, and your soul's purpose. While the Eternal Self holds much of the soul's wisdom, it isn't as concerned with trivial life happenings (because it doesn't have a strong connection with the ego), so think carefully before connecting—are you contacting your Eternal Self for a higher purpose/with pure intent? This is a sacred part of you, protected by its own generator of Love and innocence. The Eternal Self will not speak with the ego, for the ego has little understanding of such a highly stationed energy. However, the high heart and sacred heart are worthy of contact, as the heart holds within it enough Love, compassion, and openness to receive any message the Eternal Self shares. Remember, the Eternal Self is one of the highest, purest, and finest energetic aspects of you. Treat this energy with humility, and be open to receiving only messages or healings the Eternal Self deems appropriate.

It is advisable to connect with your heart space before working with any Light Code, as this allows the greatest potential of energies to connect and flow through you. However, with this Light Code, connecting with your heart space is essential, so as you work with Potakama, think of someone or something you love or care deeply about.

Sit comfortably with your back straight. Begin with the usual grounding practice at the beginning of this book. You may wish to include the Six Direction Meditation as it will help you enter a deeper meditative state.

Place one or both hands over your heart space. Slow your breath. Imagine breathing with your heart, expanding the heart space on the inhale, and contracting it on the exhale. Continue until you feel a good connection with your heart space. Imagine and feel the energy from your heart space filling your entire body with each breath. When you're ready, as you exhale, imagine and feel that you are expanding this energy out of every pore. Fill the room you're sitting in with the heart energy radiating from you. Your heart draws your Love to you with each inhale, and each exhale releases the energy into the surrounding space. Once you feel the energy flowing with ease, quietly say to yourself, "My heart, please come forward and take my hands." Breathe here for a few moments until you feel as though your heart is embracing your hands (which are still on your chest). Next, gaze gently upon the Light Code. Continue to breathe slowly and deeply, connected to your heart space. Allow the Light Code energies to wash over you and touch your heart.

You may choose to complete your meditation here or continue.

With the energies of the Code connected to your heart, ask the Light Code to assist your heart and conscious mind to connect you with your Eternal Self. Imagine and feel your heart expanding, following the energies of the Light Code to your Eternal Self. Breathe. Communicate with your Eternal Self as invited. When you are complete, thank your Eternal Self for meeting with you. Then thank your heart, the Light Code, and your guidance. You may work with this meditation and Light Code whenever you feel moved to do so.

Yawaetama

(Ya-wae-ta-ma)
SOUL WITHIN THE GODHEAD

All souls are held within the divine,
sacred energetic space and consciousness
of the Supreme: the Godhead.

My dear, the Godhead is your home. For some people, knowing this will offer relief, as many struggle to feel at ease on the earth plane. For those who feel displaced, misunderstood, or uncomfortable as an incarnated being on Gaia, this truth will be welcome. You are no longer lost. There is no need to feel homesick, or as though it was a mistake to experience a life on Earth.

It is common for people to feel as though they don't belong or are unwanted or unneeded. Whether this comes from past or present, family, friends, or community; the workplace, school, or culture; or from your country, many people feel disconnected to those around them. It's a lonely place to be, and the feelings can become the driving force for making poor choices that are out of alignment with one's higher aspects (such as collecting unnecessary programs, traumas, addictions, or karmic ties). Releasing such energetic dynamics through healing and growth strengthens our ability to tune into Truth. Our perceptive abilities open to see through the quagmire, and we find ourselves ready to receive the energies and messages from this Light Code.

Perhaps we wonder why we didn't discover the energies of this Code earlier—it might have offered us protection from our own misgivings. But we remind ourselves: *trust the journey*. No matter what you have been through, there is always a positive, because every experience shows you who you are and who you are not. The more you discover about yourself, the more easily you can connect with your soul. Step by step and leap by leap, you work your way into a deeper connection with your higher aspects. Eventually, you read this message and prepare yourself to connect with your soul in a new way. Not only can you feel your higher aspects offering comfort, but when you are introduced to the higher aspects held within the great Love of the God-head, you see everything from a new perspective. Every step that takes you closer to the Godhead offers something special, even if it's just the profound simplicity of peace.

The connection begins when our higher self facilitates a conscious relationship with our soul. As we establish our soul awareness, our ability to interact with our higher self becomes easier, creating the circular "ramping up" of energy and connectivity that is necessary for discovering further touch points in the infinite realms of consciousness.

The higher self does a wonderful job for us in relating to finer and more dignified energies. We understand a greater picture of ourselves, the world, and the relationship between the two. As we grow in consciousness and awareness, we can tune in to the energies of our soul. By the time we connect with our soul, we accept the world differently.

We feel gratitude for our experiences, even those we prefer not to have had. All of this prepares us for our continued journey in expansion and higher consciousness. Eventually, we broaden our frequency range to become aware of the Godhead: our soul's true home.

When you are ready, do the preparatory grounding exercise at the beginning of this book. Take your time. Get grounded. Feel the energy moving easily and freely up your body. Then do the Six Direction Meditation, and expand your awareness to include the edge of your aura. Finish by returning to your heart space. Next, gaze upon the Light Code. Breathe slowly and deeply, breathing in the energies of the Code. Say its name, "Yawaetama" (Ya-wae-ta-ma) three times out loud, connecting with the sound vibration. What other senses can you use to connect with the energy of the symbol? While breathing deeply and meditating upon Yawaetama, feel the edges of your aura and your heart space. Welcome the energies as they come to you. Stay with the experience for as long as you feel guided. When you finish, thank Yawaetama for its help and thank the Beings of Love and Light who assist you.

Toohlaruma

(Tooh-la-ru-ma)
CONNECTING WORLDS

*The human brain is a complex,
interconnected network that mirrors
cosmic and galactic systems.*

A s part of conscious expansion, we are required to make
new connections on the micro and macro levels of our
awareness. When human beings seek to make greater
connections to all things, we are asking to grow in a multitude of ways. To continue growing, some people will need
to expand their mind to connect with and integrate fresh
energies and information from different cosmic locations
or dimensions.

The human brain mirrors the cosmic web of the universe with its interconnected network of neurons. Have
you ever experienced a spark-like energy in your brain
when a new idea resonates with you, or you learn a new
concept? We can experience a powerful moment like this
when we have a stimulating conversation with someone
and something they say triggers a "light bulb" or "ah-ha!"
moment for us. An idea emerges, and suddenly we have a
cascade of insights about a notion or energy which, only

a moment ago, was illusive or intangible. This new connection creates a bridge between our old and new thought patterns. That bridge is like a superhighway carrying information we can use whenever we need it. We can develop the skill to connect to points in the cosmos as we choose to gain knowledge, information, or insight. There are millions of potential cosmic, world, and planetary contact points available, depending on our individual desire, direction, or interest.

Toohlaruma is a symbol for the mental plane and has many functions. An individual's interests and their soul's life mission will determine their experience of (and use of) this symbol. This intriguing Light Code creates a spark of energy that is generated on our mental plane. The energy is released into the infinite potential of timelines and dimensions, assisting us with integrating new cosmic and galactic contact points. You can think of this Code as equivalent to having a stimulating conversation with someone. You can use this symbol for meditations involving astral travel and waking dreams. It can help you break through barriers, jump timelines and dimensions, and connect with your star family. This Code acts as a portal to other worlds, as directed by the seeker's consciousness or spirit guides.

Toohlaruma is also a technological Code, meaning that it can assist us on the mental plane by helping us integrate and expand our capacity to receive new energetic technical information. Besides working as a portal to access an expanded array of information on a topic (as all Light Codes do), technological Codes like Toohlaruma also offer information technology from the cosmic and galactic planes. Toohlaruma's offerings can be specific or broad, depending on the receiver's interest and soul purpose.

Your higher aspects and guidance will help you determine how you work with this Light Code. Even if you are not called to expand your mind on additional cosmic levels, it is still important to grow in your consciousness and awareness. Focus on internal energies for optimal brain function with this Light Code, to build elasticity and neuro-connections in the brain, and to stimulate learning, etc. If you would like to expand your reach to new levels of the cosmic scale, this Light Code will help. You alone direct and determine the action or inaction of the Toohlaruma.

Working with Toohlaruma can activate of all your chakras, with a focus on the root, solar plexus, heart, third eye, and crown. Toohlaruma helps establish a portal to a specific contact point. After making a new contact, there is a collection and focusing of fresh energy. Over time, meditating (or other processes of your choice) reveals new contact points, energy, and information to your conscious mind. More will become known to the conscious mind over time with technological Codes, especially as we are ready physically, mentally, and emotionally, to comprehend and anchor these connections.

Prior to meditating with this symbol, set your intention. Decide whether you want to focus the energy inward, or if you want to focus your energy outward (such as to astral travel, discover other realms or worlds, make connections with different external energies, etc.). Once you have decided, make your verbal declaration with an affirmation such as, "I choose to . . .," and then make your request.

When you are ready, use the grounding meditation at

the beginning of this book. Relax. Gaze upon the Light Code. Breathe deeply. Breathe in the energies of the Code. How do you feel? Do you feel drawn to go deeper? If so, close your eyes. Focus back on your heart and breath. Ask the Light Code to show you what you are ready, willing, and able to receive as it pertains to the intention set at the beginning of this meditation. This may not be a visual or conscious experience—you may need to rely on your intuition. You may only receive information on the subconscious levels until your being is ready to work with it in your waking life. Once you feel complete, thank Toohlaruma and the guides who love and support you for their help.

Lakumatra

(La-ku-ma-tra)
CONSCIOUS CONNECTION TO DNA

*Every bit of DNA we hold within
our body is there for a purpose.*

Our DNA holds a great deal of information. In fact, the physical body is like a library of the entire universe! Each of us holds in infinite form within our being everything that is, was, will be, and can be. Deepening our conscious connection with our structural DNA is a powerful step toward strengthening our authority and divine power.

Lakumatra's energy is closely related to—and a higher expression of—the Light Code Panma, from *The Little Book of Light Codes*. Like Panma, Lakumatra relates to the movement of Light and the expansion of frequencies. Panma (*moving with Light, expanding frequencies*) is an introductory Code for a broader concept of how we can experience a physical life from the perspective of a photon. Panma provides a practical life lesson on how to be more like Light, as Light can be a particle or a wave. Panma shares that the consequences of navigating life through a wounded ego are akin to the way something solid makes impact with another solid: traumatically. We can learn how to experience life more like a wave, bending, reflecting, refracting, and going with the flow (as opposed to bumping up against something). Panma suggests we can learn to navigate life in the same way light waves and light particles do, especially since we are Beings of Light!

Now, with Lakumatra, we take this concept deeper by applying wave potential to our DNA. Light is stored within our being and in the potential of greater consciousness. When two particles are connected in the quantum field such that if we spin one particle, the other particle spins as well, even if they are placed a great distance apart, quantum physics says these two particles are "entangled." Our challenge is to bring our awareness to a level at which we realize the quantum connection of all things within our being. We have autonomy, free will, and choice, and within our beings, on energetic and physical levels, we hold all potentiality.

Every bit of DNA coding we hold within our bodies is there for a purpose, whether it is active or appears to be dormant. Dormant DNA holds the frequency of information, even though it may not appear to be playing an active role in the physical body's function. Perhaps inactive DNA is an active placeholder for energy, a potential transmitter of sorts, awaiting deeper connections in consciousness. This connection may unveil layers of potential knowledge, wisdom, and information for the individual and the collective consciousness. Some of this potential might manifest as gifts and talents or as an ability to connect deeply with Self, Spirit, or other beings. It might broaden your sensory perception, or you might receive information you could not otherwise process, and so on.

Working with this Light Code will be a long-term practice, as it is important for you to connect with your DNA slowly. Activating DNA may influence the physical body, so it's wise to implement these changes slowly so we remain gentle and honoring of our sacred vessel.

Meditate upon the Code as you normally do, using the grounding meditation at the beginning of this book. When you feel Earth's energy moving up into your body, draw your focus within. Gaze upon Lakumatra as you move Earth's energy throughout your body. Ask the Light Code and your spirit guides to assist you in connecting with the DNA strands that it is in your best and highest interest to connect with. Imagine, feel, and sense your DNA. Remain open to how you might sense your DNA. Can you tell which ones seem active, and which ones seem inactive? Perhaps you notice a sensation or see light in one area but not another. Ask the symbol and your spirit guides to assist you in bringing more of your consciousness stream into some of the quiet or inactive DNA strands. Imagine, feel, and sense the symbol being absorbed into those strands. From within the strands, you may perceive a subtle glow. Breathe with the glow, and notice that it becomes brighter with every breath. A quiet or inactive strand will eventually have as much (or more) Light within and around it as the other DNA strands.

Only go through this process once every thirty days or more. Trust that whatever you perceived in your session was waking you to a new level of awareness. Bring your attention back to the grounding practice and when you are ready, open your eyes if you have closed them. Thank the symbol and your spirit guides for their help.

Manoka

(Ma-no-ka)

TELOMERE REPAIR

*The health of the telomere and our connection
to Self are in direct relationship with one
another, mirroring our physical vitality
with our harmonic resonance with the world.*

Progressively, as the physical body holds more Light, the more energy our body has at its disposal to heal, repair, and connect with Source. Nurturing and developing our physical body's ability to hold a greater range of Light frequencies affects the body in ways we may be conscious of (such as improved sleep quality and a well-regulated nervous system), and unconsciously (such as being less vulnerable to disease and decay).

From a scientific perspective, the division of a cell might disturb the integrity of DNA within a chromosome. Fortunately, our chromosomes are protected with telomeres; caps at the end of each chromosome that shield the DNA from damage.[1] As our cells divide, the length of our telomeres shortens over time, until eventually they cannot replicate. The length of our telomeres correlates directly

---

1   *Gregg Braden, March 2022, https://www.youtube.com/watch?v=NBXYSWOEGno.

with our ability to live a long and healthy life.

From a metaphysical perspective, telomeres also act like antennas at the end of a chromosome, broadcasting energetic information to all the cells in our bodies. The more energy the telomeres give and receive, the more energy the body has for functioning and healing. As our telomeres hold more Light, they can share harmonious energy throughout the body. They can also transmit sound vibration to other cells. Listening to harmonic music and sound vibrations in resonance with the universe, such as solfeggio frequencies, crystal singing bowls, and tuning forks, is healing to the body. Telomeres receive sound vibrations and help reverberate the beneficial signal throughout the body, supporting a global harmonic resonance throughout the physical body.

Telomeres could be called enlightenment-meres, because of their importance in the physical relationship with Source energy. Our telomeres need repair because of repetitive traumas and exposure to toxins (from simply living on this planet, and certain lifestyle choices) which distort our connection with the authentic self and Source. It is important, therefore, that we rebuild our telomeres, and understand that the closer we are in resonance with our self, the healthier our telomeres become. The healthier our telomeres, the more Light they hold, and the better our alignment is with our authentic self and Source. There is a direct relationship between the self, our emotional world, and the health of the telomere. Healing ancestral lines and our own shadows will reduce our emotional volatility, which can also increase the vitality and life force of the telomeres and the physical body. This increased vitality translates to better health and happiness with a high vibration.

To work with this Light Code, you will need a mantra that resonates with you, such as, "I choose to heal and repair all of my telomeres to their original divine design." Once you have your mantra, set it aside and begin your practice by referring to the grounding meditation at the beginning of this book. When you feel grounded, say your mantra for three minutes while gazing upon the Light Code. Then release the mantra and gaze upon the Light Code, breathing in the healing energies being directed to your telomeres. Imagine, feel, and sense the energy from the earth and the energy from the symbol repairing and revitalizing all your telomeres. When you feel complete, thank the Light Code, your body, and Spirit for their help.

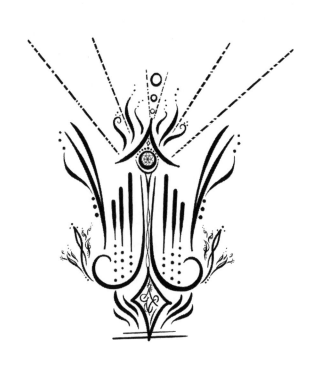

Hanatoka

(Ha-na-to-ka)

INNER TEMPLE

*Without a solid, conscious connection with
the inner temple, happiness and joy are fleeting.*

The inner temple is the root of our physical existence combined with the energies of Source, our higher aspects, and our Eternal Self. This is not a "location" within the physical body, but an accumulation of energies which occur naturally within the physical and energetic bodies. It is a space where we find comfort, peace, and answers to many of life's questions. The energies of the inner temple are mysterious, as for most of humanity, they are hidden or distorted. However, for those seekers who choose to step into their divine power and authority, it is not only possible to locate one's inner temple, it is necessary. The inner temple is an aspect of our center, a description of the soul manifested. It is the energy which defines and describes us as an incarnated personality, and it is the place where our entire being's energy congregates. Strengthening our connection to our Inner Temple will assist in us in improving our manifestation skills, as it's difficult to manifest without a conscious connection to this space. Happiness and joy can be fleeting without a solid, conscious connection with the inner temple, as well.

To become consciously aware of the inner temple, we must be humble. We must connect with our heart and have a desire to be greater than who we are right now. Our lower self must be willing to bow down to the sacred energies and teachings of this space, releasing what we thought we knew, and being willing to gain truth in new ways. This can be difficult, especially for people who haven't done enough inner healing work, or if the ego-mind is strong. However, we encourage everyone to connect with this inner temple.

A vast, eternal energy, the inner temple lives within one's seven major chakras, and is also a divine location as an aspect of the soul. It is anchored in the root, sacral, solar plexus, heart, and throat chakras, as a more physical aspect. While the third eye and crown chakras are a part of the inner temple, they are connected with its energies on a soul level. Because many people struggle with grounding, the lower chakras are typically less connected to the Inner Temple. Learning how to ground and move energy through the body effectively, and healing the energies associated with the seven energy centers are all important skills for strengthening our connection to the Inner Temple.

It is common for our chakras to be out of alignment from simply living life—it's a natural hazard of the human experience. Ultimately, we seek to align the seven major energy centers so that they spin appropriately and move energy efficiently. To engage fully with the energy and consciousness of the inner temple, all seven chakras need to be functioning well. The inner temple is like a gem hidden within our chakras and soul until we have healed ourselves and aligned to our truth. Only then can we access it. So, we may need to do more inner work in order to become proficient in aligning the chakras and raising our vibrations.

To work with this symbol, focus on moving your breath straight up your body, from your root to your crown. Tune in to how easily your breath can move up the center of your body, and when you feel as though the energy is flowing freely, move on to the next step. It may take several minutes to feel the energy flow as your chakras come into alignment. When you feel ready, bring your focus to your heart space. Breathe Earth's energy through your body as you do the preparatory grounding meditation at the beginning of this book. When you are ready, bring your attention to your root, sacral, and solar plexus chakras, while still connecting with the heart center. Breathe deeply. There's no rush. In your timing, gaze upon the Light Code and ask to be guided to your inner temple. It may be helpful to close your eyes once you feel a connection with the Light Code. If you have trouble connecting with your inner temple, be patient. Breathe deeply, or try again another day. When you make contact, you may feel a rise of energy, and potentially a more empowered mindset. What you feel, sense, and perceive will be unique to you. This space is comforting, eternal, and may feel like "home." When you are complete, thank the energies of the Light Code and your guidance for their help.

Yarimarwae

(Ya-re-mar-wae)
KINGDOM OF HEAVEN

*The Kingdom of Heaven is a
beautiful space representing the energy
of your Being and true home.*

There was a time on this Earth when souls were free to come and go from this plane as they wished. Many souls wanted to experience a life on Gaia because of its incredible beauty and its 3D density. When a soul experiences a life within this density, there is more physical sensation and feedback than there is in higher dimensions, therefore there is greater potential to learn and experience.

Playing with our six senses, relationship dynamics, and light and dark energies are all wonderful parts of being human. Many incarnated souls are intrigued by lower vibrational "dark" energies, and there are important dynamics between light and dark vibrations about which we can learn. The lower vibrational dark energies were (and still are) alluring and confusing. Lower vibrational energies can be powerful, and can manipulate lower aspects of the self to act out of accordance with Love. Souls are curious, and engage with a range of energies, sometimes of their own choosing, and sometimes through coercion or force. Most souls associate with dark energies at some point, creating karmic entanglements that all souls on this planet continue to work through today. The beings who are incarnated on Gaia now are either tied to Gaia karmically, or they are here to help heal dysfunctional karmic relationships. A soul chooses, both prior to birth and during a life cycle, certain karmic lines to work through in a lifetime, to resolve and neutralize karmic energies. These energetic entanglements are complex and can create what some refer to as a *soul trap*, thus distorting the natural death and rebirth process. Even souls who have had minimal lifetimes on Gaia are subject to soul trap entanglements. There are energetic "locations" within the Kingdom of Heaven that are inaccessible for complete rejuvenation while a soul is trapped in the reincarnation cycle with Gaia, hence the excessive fatigue many beings feel while incarnated.

It is important to become aware of our soul trap entanglements to begin connecting with the sacred and holy energies of the Kingdom. Yarimarwae (along with most of the Light Codes found in this book) can assist us in discovering and consciously releasing our soul trap entanglements. Working with this Light Code can also help you connect with the Kingdom of Heaven (or Authentic Kingdom, as it is sometimes called) by reducing the pull or intensity of the soul trap. The Kingdom of Heaven is the sacred space where parts of the soul connect to relax, clear, process energies, and rejuvenate. Once connected to the Kingdom, one will be able to freely choose with their free will whether to enter the Kingdom of Heaven when they leave this dimension and world at death. Otherwise, one will most likely return to this plane to learn and utilize another opportunity to complete their karmic work.

Let us be clear, the above understanding is not something to evoke fear. This is an offering for clarity and empowerment and contains a cautionary note: If you do not want to reincarnate in a future lifetime, you must truly Love this planet, neutralize your karmic energies, and be willing to return. It doesn't mean you will return, but you must be willing to return. This dynamic is a paradoxical part of healing the cycle of the soul trap.

This Light Code holds the energy of the rest-and-rejuvenation location within the Kingdom of Heaven that is not entangled with the earth plane. If you feel great soul fatigue, this Light Code can support you. Otherwise, you may use this Code to connect with the Kingdom of Heaven and state your decisions with regard to your reincarnation cycles. You may choose to reincarnate, but it will be your choice. The current energies of our Earth and solar system that we are working with now provide an easier transition and touch point to the Authentic Kingdom. It is now much clearer for you and your loved ones to choose if reincarnation is appropriate for them. Please understand that if you choose to release yourself from the entangled karmic cycle, you, as a spirit, will still be able to guide and assist your loved ones. You will not abandon those you care about, as the bands of Love formed on this planet, or any other, are eternal. You are always connected in profound ways that the human body can feel only fractionally.

You can connect with the Authentic Kingdom through meditating and gazing upon

Yarimarwae. It may also be profound to include this symbol during plant medicine ceremonies, such as a cacao ceremony. Accessing this energy while still inhabiting a human body provides a wonderful healing opportunity. You can fall asleep while meditating on this Code for enhanced rejuvenation time and dream time. Because of its sacred nature, we recommend you create a mini-ceremony when you work with this Light Code. Perhaps build a small altar, light a candle (if not falling asleep and while using common fire safety sense), state your intentions or requests, offer gratitude for the process, and begin your meditation. If you don't fall asleep when you are finished, thank the symbol and Spirit for their help. Always allow the candle to burn out if possible.

Ka-ahara

(Ka aha-ra)
CONSCIOUS EMBODIMENT
OF THE INFINITE

*Step into the magnificent, balanced
consciousness of the Infinite.*

Life challenges us constantly. How we respond reflects how balanced, connected, and clear we are in our hearts and minds. The healing and spiritual tools and practices we gather assist us in expanding our consciousness and awareness as we move closer to our true nature and the Divine. Step by step, we embrace the coherent energy of our Love, and the magnificent, grounded energies of the Infinite.

The Infinite is an aspect of our Holy Self, an aspect of Source, and a divine expression offered to all facets of our being. It is a flourishing of one's energies, magnified and manifested across all realms and timelines. Our conscious connection to the Infinite offers possibilities and opportunities, some of which are created and witnessed in life, such as through synchronicities and miraculous events. Developing a practice (such as working with this Light Code) to engage with the Infinite from a grounded, positive, and coherent space is essential to embodying this powerful energy.

Ka-ahara is especially useful for the lower parts of ourselves that require healing and can bring greater awareness and wholeness. The unhealed parts of us call out in times of stress, when we are uninspired, lacking in Love, or in need of forgiveness. We remain blissfully unaware of these energies until something triggers them, provoking the need for acknowledgment, balance, and release. Sometimes, we know we must release energies, but we can have difficulty pinpointing them. Identifying lower vibrational energies provides a positive opportunity to release what no longer serves our highest outcome.

This Light Code assists us in contacting lower aspects and energies. Its purpose is not only to shed light on our shadows, but also to lift those parts of ourselves that need to be elevated. Sometimes, in order to move past something, all we need is to be seen and heard, and this is another way Ka-ahara can assist. This symbol is connected with Kuan Yin, the mother of compassion. If you feel a strong connection with this symbol, maybe Kuan Yin is greeting you!

You may use this symbol to raise your vibration across all levels of your being, for while it can target the lower aspects of the self, it is not limited to any frequency or dimension. In fact, this symbol has an incredible range— it can connect with our lowest, incoherent, unbalanced aspects, right up to our highest divine expressions of Love. Ka-ahara works independently from other Codes but can work well with "Embodiment of Infinite Potential" (Kumara'aha) and "Conscious Connection to DNA" (Lakumatra). All three symbols assist you in connecting with your potential.

To work with Ka-ahara, please follow the suggested meditation at the beginning of the book, or take this Light Code
into Fractalline Healing or other favorite meditation for
further exploration. Breathe the symbol's energy into your
being for as long as you feel is appropriate. When you are
finished, thank Ka-ahara and the Beings of Love and Light
who assist you.

Ya-aharwae

(Ya ahar-wae)

GODHEAD

*This great consciousness is a home
to you, offering everything you could
ever require to be in your Truest Self.*

This Light Code holds the energy of the Godhead, so you can more easily connect with this space deep within yourself. Dear one, we offer you a hand, to take you to a place you already reside, a place so pure of Love that it shines golden white from high above. You come here in between lifetimes, and occasionally while you sleep, to rejuvenate and reconnect to the Infinite, Eternal Truths. The Godhead is an energy, a space, and a consciousness. It is somewhere to visit, but it is also somewhere to be at all times. This great consciousness is a home to you, offering everything you could ever require to be in your Truest Self. It is a manifestation of Universal Source energy, and it is also you. This interconnected oneness of highest integrity, honor, and Love is where we go when we need to remember what is greater than ourselves. It offers perspective and holiness that reaches to the depths of our being and soul. Its grace calls forth the grace within you, so you walk this plane with consciousness, wisdom, and beauty. Use Ya-aharwae when you are in need of faith and a deeper connection to your Love. You can connect with the energy of the Godhead when you are seeking refuge, comfort, or guidance.

This symbol not only holds the frequencies and energetic signatures of the Godhead, but it acts as a portal to the divine consciousness of the Godhead. The Godhead is of a very high vibration, and over time, as you increase your own vibration, you will experience "location" changes as the space reveals itself to you. Remain open and notice how this sacred consciousness offers itself to you every time you connect. Trust that what you receive is most appropriate for you now. As with all the Light Codes offered in this book, you can use this Code by gazing at it, or you may choose to follow the meditation below.

Some people will read the meditation below and experience its benefits with their eyes open. Others will need to read the meditation first, then close their eyes and move into the practice. Please choose the best option for you.

Begin by using the Grounding meditation and Six Direction Meditation at the beginning of this book. When you are ready, gaze for a moment upon Ya-aharwae. Imagine and feel you are being lifted higher than you have ever gone before. See, sense, and feel Earth getting smaller, and the light around you getting brighter. You are weightless, and your ascent is smooth. Feel yourself drifting ever higher into brighter and brighter light. Feel the surrounding energy. Eventually, you will find yourself surrounded by a golden light. Allow yourself to relax and rest in this space. You may have questions—ask them. Feel gratitude welling up in your heart space and being shared naturally with the Godhead. When you feel complete, begin your descent. Feel yourself moving down through the light as the energy becomes denser. Gravity becomes noticeable, and your breath deepens. Tune in to your body and the space you around you. When you are ready, open your eyes. Blink. Notice where you are, and feel grateful for the incredible gift it is to be human. Offer gratitude to Ya-aharwae, your spirit guides, Source, and yourself.

Epilogue

We each have an important mission, or perhaps multiple missions, to accomplish in our life. Some of us create products, others offer help in some fashion, but we all play a role in the workings of society in one form or another. By reading this book, you have done yourself and humanity a great service. You've taken some of your precious life moments to dedicate to your own self-exploration and development. You've searched for clarity, honored your sacred nature, and expanded parts of yourself that were waiting for the call. For this, I am both humbled and deeply touched. It is a pleasure to share the powerful Universal Light Codes with you, and I hope they will continue to serve you and those you love for decades.

All blessings on your continued unfolding as the beautiful Light Being That You Are,

LAARA

Afterword

With a full heart of gratitude, I cannot help but marvel at the profound impact of this book on its readers. Each of you has embarked on a transformative journey, one that promises to enhance your self-awareness and illuminate your life experiences.

Let me take a moment to express my utmost appreciation for Laara, whose expertise and meticulous approach shine brightly throughout this remarkable book. From the outset, she masterfully lays the groundwork, delving into the history and significance of Light Codes, offering valuable insights into their benefits, and providing us with foundational meditations that effortlessly pave the way for our exploration. With Laara as our guide, we are set to embark on a wondrous voyage of experiencing the Codes firsthand.

As we venture deeper into the realms of the Light Codes, we may notice that their digestibility varies. Some Codes invite us to effortlessly immerse ourselves in their essence, resonating with our very being. It is as if these codes find an immediate home within us, igniting a profound connection. Yet, there are others that present a delightful challenge, inviting us to stretch our boundaries and explore the depths of their meaning.

Initially, I found myself attempting to decipher the reasons behind this varying experience. My logical mind sought to justify my preferences, assuming that certain Codes were more aligned with my needs or resonated with my soul on a profound level. However, as I journeyed through the book, a newfound understanding emerged: the Light Codes hold layers of meaning that extend far beyond our immediate comprehension. It is through continued exploration and engagement with these Codes that we unlock new insights, connections, and dimensions of understanding. With this realization, I am filled with excitement at the prospect of revisiting these Codes time and again, to witness the different hues of light they unveil.

As we repeatedly delve into the vastness of these Light Codes, their energy gracefully imprints upon our very being, and they integrate themselves into the fabric of our existence. Through this integration, we are filled with the profound information carried within the light, igniting a radiant transformation within ourselves. We become conduits of light, illuminating our perception of self, others, and the harmonized reality that surrounds us.

In Traditional Chinese Medicine, there exists a concept known as "guwen, " often translated as "ancient script." However, its deeper meaning lies in the "transmission of the ancients." It teaches us that when we acquire knowledge that proves helpful, we are honor-bound to share it with others. Such sharing is based on the belief that knowledge is a precious gift, one that should be extended to benefit all.

In this spirit, I implore you to embark on a continued exploration of not only this book but also the vast body of work that Laara has crafted. As she progresses on her own journey of sharing her divine insights, I invite you to share your own experiences, reflections, and discoveries with others. Let us collectively bask in the radiant light of these Codes, ensuring that their transformative power reaches far and wide.

May your journey with the Light Codes be one of profound self-discovery, growth, and connection. Embrace the boundless wisdom they offer and allow their radiance to illuminate your path, as we venture together toward a more vibrant and enlightened existence.

With gratitude and a deep knowing that the light within us all is ever-expanding.

RA OF EARTH

References

Braden, Gregg. Gregg Braden's Official YouTube Channel. March 21, 2022. *HUMAN Chromosome 2 & The Theory of EVOLUTION… Mysterious Intervention* [Video]. YouTube. https://www.youtube.com/watch?v=NBXYSWOEGno.

Green, Glenda. *Love Without End—Jesus Speaks*. Sedona: Spiritus, 1999.

About
the Author

Laara is a spiritual mentor, healing practitioner, and author of *The Little Book of Light Codes* and *Light Codes for the Soul*. She is a graduate of the Healing Light Center Church's Crucible Program, having earned degrees in Master of Healing Arts and Master of Natural Theology in Sacred Healing. Laara is also the developer of the innovative quantum healing modality, Fractalline Healing™. She offers workshops, online courses, and her YouTube channel, which features spiritual wisdoms and Light Language channeling. She dedicates her life to assisting those who choose to align to their soul's purpose and power, connect with Light Language, and learn spiritual principles. When she isn't channeling or teaching, Laara can be found playing with her cats, riding her horse, or practicing her handstands.

Made in the USA
Columbia, SC
19 November 2024

46962094R00124